# MIND DRUGS

## SIXTH EDITION

# MIND DRUGS

## SIXTH EDITION

## By Margaret O. Hyde

with Duke D. Fisher, M.D.
Elizabeth Forsyth, M.D.
Allan Y. Cohen, Ph.D.

The Millbrook Press
Brookfield, Connecticut

TO EMILY, MOLLY, AND BEN

Library of Congress Cataloging-in-Publication Data
Hyde, Margaret O. (Margaret Oldroyd).
Mind drugs, sixth edition / by Margaret O. Hyde with Duke D.
Fisher, Elizabeth Forsyth, Allan Y. Cohen. — 6th ed.
p. cm.
Rev. ed. of: Mind drugs / edited by Margaret O. Hyde.
5th ed. © 1986.
Includes bibliographical references and index.
Summary: Leading authorities on drugs discuss the use, abuse,
and the effects of marijuana, alcohol, LSD, heroin, cocaine,
PCP, and other drugs and the alternatives to drug use.
ISBN 0-7613-0970-5 (lib. bdg.)
1. Substance abuse—United States—Juvenile literature. 2.
Youth—Substance use—United States—Juvenile literature.
[1. Drugs. 2. Drug abuse.] I. Title.
HV4999.2.M56 1998
613.8—dc21 98-20392 CIP AC

Published by The Millbrook Press, Inc.
2 Old New Milford Road, Brookfield, Connecticut 06804

# Contents

# MIND DRUGS

# SIXTH EDITION

# 1

# The Mind Drug Supermarket

*Margaret O. Hyde*

**T**he world is well stocked with mind drugs. From the geek to the cool kid, from the unborn to the elderly, the poor to the rich, the conservative to the liberal, and all the people in between, mind-altering drugs, legal and illegal, are part of the lives of many Americans.

Courtney is a drug abuser who drinks ten cups of coffee a day, which causes her indigestion. Leo's parents drink wine with dinner and find it a very pleasant experience. Vera's pill popping led to her suicide. Michael's alcohol abuse caused a vehicular homicide.

The drug store for chemicals that affect the mind has grown into a giant supermarket. Cocaine may be cited in today's fatal crash on the highway; meth (methamphetamine) has moved from the heartland to many parts of the United States as a drug of choice; marijuana is the subject of a current government controversy; nicotine and alcohol make the headlines frequently.

Mind drugs are sniffed, swallowed, injected, and smoked for relaxation, to escape problems, to combat depression, to achieve status, or just out of curiosity. An estimated $200 to $300 million changes hands in drug deals every day in the United States.[1] Addicts are getting sick and dying at record rates.[2] Epidemics of drug abuse rage through cities, suburbs, sleepy towns, and rural America. Still, in the midst of the heaviest drug scenes, some children are growing up drug-free.[3]

---

**DRUG SCENE**

Ten children live in an abandoned house for two weeks after their drug-abusing parents leave them there. They survive by stealing water, using the electricity from an empty house next door, eating what they can get from the food shelf at the local church, and huddling together in the cold. The older children manage to go to school, where they get free breakfast and lunch. When a neighbor reports the smell of kerosene in the "empty" house, police arrive and see two drug users fleeing from the building. Inside, they find the children. The children are taken to foster homes.

---

The amount of drug abuse varies with individual choice, environment, and the knowledge of what drugs do. Not everyone abuses drugs, even though it seems that way in some neighborhoods. In the United States, most 12- to 17-year-olds have never tried marijuana, over 90 percent have never used cocaine, and about 98 percent have not used crack within the last year. Between 1995 and 1996, the percentage of eighth graders reporting daily use of alcohol was 1 percent. But for many teens, smoking marijuana is part of a daily routine.[4] A report issued at the end of 1997 indicated that drug use among eighth graders had stopped climbing for the first time in more than five years, but older students reported smoking marijuana in increasing numbers.[5]

Most teens want to keep their edge. While they know that many people try drugs and walk away without apparent harm, they know that many others do not escape their drug experience unscathed. Crack and methamphetamine users are more easily addicted than most alcohol and marijuana users, but the risk of addiction varies with many factors besides the drug itself.

New research has spread light on how drugs manipulate the brain's stress and reward systems to keep users coming back for more. Authorities agree that regular use of any intoxicant that blurs reality and encourages a kind of psychological escapism makes growing up more difficult. But who is an authority? While some users and abusers are well versed in the language of the street, their knowledge of what a certain amount of a drug will do to the nervous system of a human being is slim. To them, the uniqueness of individual physical reactions remains a total mystery. Such self-styled authorities may be unaware that what happens to one person who takes a drug may be very different from what happens to another.

In addition, the way a drug acts on any mind varies with the amount of the dose, the conditions under which it is taken, the purity of the dose, the user's health, and other factors. And in the underground, the true contents of drugs are often unknown. Awareness of the above is increasing among young people who are exposed to the world of illegal drugs, but the overall number who believe there is danger in taking drugs is decreasing.[6]

Some kids are really tired of hearing about drug abuse on TV, at school, on posters in subways and buses, at home, and just about everywhere. What can you believe? The old scare tactics based on ignorance and fear have been largely discarded in favor of facts and research programs aimed at learning more of the truth about drugs.

Drug abuse runs in cycles, with the amount of use depending on various factors, including knowledge. By the end of 1997, the worst of the crack epidemic appeared to be over. Young people who had witnessed the ravages of crack looked down on "crackheads." While older users continued, or died from drugs (or from gun violence), fewer kids started using crack and the market declined.[7]

If you are informed about mind drugs, you can make knowledgeable decisions both about your own use or nonuse and about the future of American drug policy. The clouds that surround the area of drug abuse have hardly begun to clear. There are no easy answers. Perhaps there are still more questions than answers, but the situation is being attacked on many fronts, including medical, social, economic, and legal.

---

**DRUG SCENE**

Christopher is exploring the drug culture on the Internet. He enjoys the trippy, groovy information that is available. Sometime he watches croaky frogs that are part of a beer ad. He knows that much online drug information is not true, and he is wary of chat lines.

---

Each drug abuser has taken his or her journey to "nowhere" for complex personal reasons. Bringing the abuser home requires many bridges, and a great deal of understanding on the part of each individual who helps. A tremendous amount of money and education of young and old are needed to encourage all people to realize that the problem of drug abuse is their problem, the problem of everyone who lives in today's world.

# 2

# Getting High Long Ago

*Margaret O. Hyde*

**G**etting high on drugs is nothing new. Drugs have been used to alter consciousness in most societies throughout history, and different drugs have been considered acceptable at different times and places.[1] Many kinds of animals were users long before humans appeared on the earth, and they continue to enjoy drugs that are found naturally. For example, pigeons enjoy marijuana seeds; elephants consume fermented palm fruit; cows, water buffalo, and antelope eat opium poppies. Reindeer enjoy mushroom highs; squirrels and birds get high on the alcohol in fermenting fruit.[2] Ornithologists testify that cedar waxwings fly great distances to enjoy the stimulation they get from eating *Pyracantha* berries. Larger birds "get loaded" on the fruit of the nutmeg tree.[3] No one knows how many different kinds of animals use drugs, but the list is growing longer as scientists learn more.

From the prehistoric humans who grew tipsy from eating fermented fruit found at the base of a tree to today's designer drug manufacturers who produce legal and illegal drugs, drug users and abusers have existed throughout history. Ronald Siegal, in his book *Intoxication: Life in the Pursuit of Artificial Passion*, maintains that the urge to alter consciousness is as basic and universal as the craving for food and sex.


## ALCOHOL: DRINK AND DRUG

Evidence of drug use by early humans appears in various places. The Bible reports that Noah "planted a vineyard and he drank of the wine and was drunken."[4] Alcohol use was widespread in Europe during primitive times.

Wine used in religious ceremonies was acceptable, but then, as today, abuse was not. While most drinkers were not abusers, there are records that show drunkenness was a problem in ancient Greece, Rome, China, Japan, and Egypt. The Egyptians wrote the following three thousand years ago:

> *Take not upon thyself to drink a jug of beer. Thou speakest, and an unintelligible utterance issueth from thy mouth. If thou fallest down and thy limbs break, there is none to hold out a hand to thee. Thy companions in drink stand up and say, "Away with this sot." And thou art like a little child.*[5]

Wine and beer were part of many celebrations and worship services through the years. In addition to being widely used for pleasure, alcohol was considered to be one of the first "wonder drugs." One English doctor in the fourteenth century hailed alcohol as a panacea for practically all of man's earthly ills.[6] Alcohol was a safer drink than the polluted water that, in early times, carried germs from person to person. And it was a friend to the man whose leg was being removed, to the woman whose teeth had to be pulled, and to all the people who were given enough of this common beverage to anesthetize them from pain.

The colonists brought alcoholic beverages with them to America from abroad, and their drinking was so common that it has been said that early America floated on alcohol. Liquid fortification was supplied in stores, on farms, at celebrations of all sorts. Many early colonists began their day with a "dose of spirits" and continued drinking at intervals throughout the day.

About a century ago, as in earlier times, alcohol was considered one of the best medicines ever known, for it was the "cure-all" in many patent and prescription medicines. Alcohol was long believed to provide strength and ward off diseases, while water was suspected of diluting body strength.

Alcohol problems were tremendous in America's history, although generally they were not considered serious until the nineteenth century. Great temperance crusades culminated in the passage of the Volstead Act in 1919, which prohibited the sale of alcoholic beverages until it was repealed in 1933. Prohibition, as it was commonly known, left a mark that still colors some individuals' attitudes on alcohol. Alcohol is now considered America's national drug.[7]

## OPIUM AND OTHER NARCOTICS

The word *narcotic* comes from a Greek word meaning "stupor," the same word that gave us our word *stupid.* But the stupor is often preceded by a wonderful feeling, known as a rush, and followed by a pleasant, dreamlike state.

While some users seek to anesthetize themselves from pain, narcotics depress brain function in a way that is different from anesthetics. They are derived from or related to opium. There are many hundreds of these opiates.[8]

Opium is a powerful drug that has been used through the ages. No one knows how long ago mothers learned to apply extract from opium poppies to their nipples to quiet their nursing babies, but opium is known as one of the oldest of all drugs.

Opium use and abuse probably originated in the Mediterranean region, where it appears to have been cultivated in Neolithic villages at least 6,000 years ago. Its medicinal properties were described in medical texts written on cuneiform tablets.

In Iraq, where ancient Sumerians lived 5,000 years ago, historians have learned that juice was extracted from a special kind of poppy known as "joy poppy" (now called the opium poppy). When dried, this juice was used to reduce pain and induce sleep. Evidence that opium was used in Egypt is found in tombs, where jars of opium were placed for use in the afterlife by people who died between 1600 and 600 B.C.

About 1000 B.C., Homer referred to the poppy plant in the *Odyssey*, where it was described as a tea. This tea was offered to travelers as a beverage of hospitality.[9] Ancient Greeks and Romans called opium a painkiller. But "joy poppies" were not cultivated in India and China before 1000 A.D., and opium smoking in the Far East did not begin until well after the fifteenth century.

Opium was used as a painkiller in Europe throughout the Middle Ages, but by then it was hard to obtain. By the eighteenth century, the use of opium was debated and more research was done to study its effects. Scientists learned how to extract from it white crystals of morphine, a drug that is used medicinally to this day.[10]

In the late eighteenth century, enterprising British, Portuguese, and American merchants discovered that they could make vast sums of money by selling opium to the Chinese. So much silver and gold was leaving China in payment for the imported opium, and so many people were becoming dependent on the drug, that China banned its use. By 1800, it was forbidden to import opium into China, but great quantities were still smuggled into the country.

The infamous Opium Wars between Great Britain and China in the mid-1800s did not solve the problem for the

Chinese. The victorious British compelled the Chinese to make restitution for damages and to allow the opium trade. By that time, Chinese farmers were producing opium at home and opium smoking had spread widely.[11]

In America, opium "dens," places where people came to smoke opium in pipes, were introduced in the West by Chinese immigrants who had been brought to this country as cheap labor to build railroads and work in gold mines. The dens played a central role in the social life of impoverished Chinese laborers. Opium smokers "hit the pipe" as often as three times a day in the dens, where they lay on couches and dreamed off the effects of the drug.

At first, only Chinese used the opium dens, but later Americans joined them. By the end of the nineteenth century, opium dens could be found in every city.[12] Smokers tended to be gamblers, prostitutes, and criminals but there were reports of "young white girls" being seduced in the dens.[13] Some of the pipe dreamers were simply interested in the thrill of doing something daring and illegal.

Across America, use of opium and its derivative, morphine, were growing. No one knows when doctors first prescribed small doses of opium to quiet crying babies and relieve pain. Paregoric, a medicine that contained opium, was used to stop infant diarrhea as well as to soothe babies.[14] Mrs. Winslow's Soothing Syrup, which contained 10 percent morphine, was widely used to soothe teething infants.

Tonics containing opium and morphine were popular, especially with women who suffered from "female troubles," and they were available without a prescription. They were recommended as cures for coughs, stomach upset, tuberculosis, whooping cough, and a long list of other ills.[15]

During the Civil War, morphine was so widely used to relieve the suffering of soldiers that morphine addiction later was called the soldier's disease.[16] The addiction that came with frequent use of opium and morphine became more widely recognized, and what had been called "God's Medicine" showed a downside. But most of the estimated million Americans who were addicted in 1890 did not know they were addicted.

Heroin, a derivative of opium, was discovered in 1898 and was heralded as a heroic painkiller. It was used in over-the-counter products for treating coughs, asthma, and other diseases.[17]

By the beginning of the twentieth century, the addictive qualities of opium and other opiates, such as heroin, codeine, laudanum, and Demerol, were a growing concern. However, so little was known about these drugs that heroin was often used in an effort to fight opium addiction.

French Corsicans and Italian-American Mafiosi played a major role in funneling opium, grown in Turkey and Southeast Asia and processed as heroin in French underground labs, to America. Mexican and Chinese gangs were active in the drug trade in the Southwest and on the West Coast. Tons of heroin reached the United States and the demand increased to epidemic proportions.[18]

## COCAINE

Cocaine is another drug that was used in the effort to break addiction to opium, morphine, and heroin. At first, this stimulant found in the leaves of the coca plant was not thought to be addictive.

The coca plant, which is thought to predate the appearance of man, thrives in South America. Thousands of years ago, workers in the Andes chewed coca leaves to lessen the discomfort of long hours of work in cold climates. In the 1890s black stevedores in New Orleans used cocaine to help endure their grueling work loading steamboats. Black laborers in other parts of the South are thought to have used cocaine as they worked on cotton plantations, railroad work camps, and construction sites.[19]

In the late 1800s, cocaine became popular in Europe both as a medicine and pleasure drug. It was a common ingredient in tonics and in "Vin Mariana," a highly successful wine that was endorsed by royalty, popes, and notable figures such as Thomas Edison, H. G. Wells, and Jules Verne.[20]

Early Coca-Cola and other beverages included cocaine as a major ingredient, but it was removed in the early 1900s. At that time laws were passed against the widespread use of coca because its dependency was recognized. (Decocainized leaves are still part of Coca-Cola's natural flavor.)

Dr. Sigmund Freud, the famous psychoanalyst, had been firmly convinced of cocaine's benefits. But by 1887, Freud called cocaine a far more dangerous enemy to health than morphine. In the beginning of the twentieth century, cocaine was outlawed for all but medicinal purposes.

## MARIJUANA

Marijuana use dates back to prehistoric times. Only one species of the plant, *Cannabis sativa*, yields both a potent drug and hemp, a strong fiber that is used in the manufacture of rope, canvas, and linen. Americans grew *Cannabis sativa* for its fiber for many years.[21]

The medical use of marijuana is not new. Five thousand years ago, the legendary Chinese Emperor Shen Nung was said to have prescribed marijuana for ailments such as gout, malaria, rheumatism, and even gas pains.[22] Until 1937, Americans considered marijuana a recognized medicine in good standing, distributed by leading pharmaceutical firms, and on sale at many pharmacies.[23]

Black slaves probably brought the knowledge of how to smoke marijuana with them to Brazil, and from there, the practice traveled to Mexico and the United States.[24] The first definite record of marijuana as a plant in the New World dates from 1545, when Spaniards introduced it from Chile.[25] Its use as an intoxicant appears to have been kept hidden by most users and was probably limited during much of the nineteenth and early twentieth centuries.

In addition to smoking marijuana, some of the more daring users tried hashish. This stronger drug, which is usually chewed or smoked, is made by drying the resin produced in the tops of female marijuana plants before the seeds form. Hashish is not as popular in the United States as marijuana, but it was part of the drug scene long ago and continues to be so, especially in India.[26]

A famous illustration of five attractive young women, exotically dressed and lying on divans, appeared in the December 2, 1876, issue of *Illustrated Police News* magazine. Water pipes were visible in this illustration of a "Hasheesh Hell," which may have been an example of the illicit places that arose following the banning of opium dens.[27]

Marijuana did not come into general use in the United States until 1920, even though it was a legal drug until 1937.[28] Although tales of the "killer weed" were spread by foes of marijuana use, stories of murder under the influence of the drug proved false. By 1967–1968, smoking marijuana became acceptable, although illegal, behavior in many high schools. One Class of 1968 was dubbed "The Class of Grass."[29] Pot parties were common, and marijuana was—and still is—easily available to students almost everywhere.

## HALLUCINOGENIC DRUGS

Hallucinogens, drugs that cause impressions of sights and sounds that are not really there, can be obtained from numerous different plant species. These drugs have been used from ancient times by peoples around the world, for they grow in forests and deserts, temperate and tropical climates. Almost always, the effect of these plants was considered mystical and religious. Indian tribes have long used "magic mushrooms" and other herbs and roots to seek a high level of mental vision. The highs these drugs produced were believed to bring users closer to the gods and to nature.[30]

The use of peyote was basic to pre-Columbian religious practices, and it spread throughout many Central American tribes to those north of Mexico, in spite of the Christian missionaries who discouraged its use. Hostility toward highs from mushrooms and other plants grew as LSD appeared on the drug scene.

LSD, lysergic acid diethylamide, was not discovered until 1938 and was not used as a hallucinogen until 1943. LSD is related to plant seeds that produce visions. The word *psychedelic* appeared in 1950 to describe combined mental and physical experiences after taking hallucinogens.

These are just some of the mind drugs that have been around for a long time. In many cases, ideas about them have changed widely. For example, in 1930, marijuana was legal and alcohol was not. Now the opposite is true. Native Americans, who were part of a culture that used peyote, did not use alcohol. According to many who study the alcohol problem among Native Americans today, peyote may have been a safer drug for them. Drug use continues to be somewhat trendy, with different drugs rising and falling in popularity.

What is called the modern drug culture appears to have started with rock musicians and other celebrities in the 1960s. Drug abuse spread to the poor in ghettos and slums, where many turned to drugs as a way to escape hopelessness and poverty. Drugs spread throughout all classes and cultures.

With drugs in general, how much, how often, and why remain important parts of the equation.

# LSD and Other Psychoactive Chemicals

*Duke D. Fisher, M.D. and Margaret O. Hyde*

*Dr. Duke D. Fisher has had extensive experience with LSD users. He is a neuropsychiatrist and was Assistant Clinical Professor of Psychiatry at the University of California School of Medicine.*

"**I** don't do drugs. I just drop acid," comments an eighth grader who collects his LSD as blotter art. He is aware that LSD is a drug, and he has a vague idea that it is illegal to possess it. He does not know that the penalty for possession of a few grams of LSD today is a minimum mandatory federal sentence of ten years. Nor does he know what LSD might do to his mind.[1]

LSD is one of many mind drugs that are known as hallucinogens. Also known as psychedelics, these drugs distort perception, cause spaciness and mild euphoria, and produce other unpredictable effects. In addition to LSD, the most common hallucinogens are marijuana, MDMA (ecstasy, rave), PCP, peyote (mescaline), and psilocybin mushrooms (schrooms).[2]

LSD became very popular on college campuses in the 1960s.[3] Today it appears to be one of the fastest-growing abused drugs among those under twenty years of age.[4]

Although the potency of LSD is generally less today than in the 1960s, users take their chances. Samples that have been analyzed range from barely detectable amounts of LSD to 500 micrograms. Any amount over 120 micrograms is regarded as extremely dangerous. No one can predict whether a trip will be good or bad.

## WHAT IS A "GOOD TRIP"?
## WHAT IS A "BAD TRIP"?

The good trip occurs if the LSD user has primarily pleasurable experiences. Some people say that they can "hear colors" and "see sounds." A trip is a highly personal experience and no two people experience it exactly alike. Some people see intense colors and have feelings that are foreign to them. Some individuals experience the feeling that their body is leaving them or that they are two people. Some people consider this drug experience to be completely unlike their previous life experiences. They believe some experiences are mystical or semireligious.

A bad trip, or "bummer," occurs when a person becomes frightened or finds the LSD-induced experience to be so unpleasant that he or she seeks help. Many bad-trippers go to hospitals, emergency rooms, counselors, or friends to get help. During the past several years many young people have reported bad trips. Physicians call bad trips adverse reactions to LSD. There have been many articles in medical journals describing some of these adverse reactions.

We started seeing many young people coming to our hospital at UCLA because of bad trips. We studied the first seventy patients who came to our emergency room to find out what kind of symptoms they had with their bad trips. The most common symptoms we found were the same as those of people suffering from a persistent psychosis, those who live in an unreal world. Some people would take LSD and their trip would continue beyond the usual twelve to eighteen hours for LSD effects. Many individuals continued to hallucinate and be paranoid—extremely suspicious with delusions of being watched, criticized, or persecuted. They were convinced that people were going to hurt them or that animals were chasing them, or they continued to be out of contact with reality.

An example of this kind of reaction was a teenage boy who locked himself in his room because he thought he was an orange and that if someone touched him, he would turn into orange juice. He was able to live because a few friends would bring in food for him; however, he remained locked in his room for several months. This type of false belief is called a delusion. We found delusions to be quite common among young people who had taken LSD.

The second most common symptom was severe depression—many times with suicidal thoughts. We talked to many young people who were convinced that they had to die because they felt so unworthy. One young girl broke a Coke bottle and cut both of her wrists after she had taken LSD at a Hollywood nightclub. Some individuals are successful in their suicide attempts.

The third most common symptom we saw in the emergency room was anxiety to the point of panic. Many people would become quite frightened at the fact that they were losing control of themselves under LSD. One college student had taken LSD and had an accident on the freeway. He was so anxious that he ran up and down the freeway until the police were able to restrain him and bring him to our hospital for treatment.

The last, most commonly observed symptom was confusion or wandering about. Many LSD users were brought to our hospital not knowing where they were going or who they were. Some of these people would be found wandering around the beaches or the city at night. Many of them were malnourished and had physical difficulties because of long exposure to the sun.

How do we treat patients with bad trips? Some of the patients were so disorganized and psychotic that long-term hospitalization was necessary. Some of the patients who were very nervous and agitated had to be given large doses of tranquilizers. Some were able to return to their families or friends after a few hours; however, it was necessary for us to hospitalize and provide longer treatment for many of the LSD users. Some bad trips would last for months, and even large doses of tranquilizers and hospitalization would not help the patient. There have been some patients who did not respond to treatment and had to be sent to state hospitals for long-term care. One young girl who took LSD was on a bad trip for four months. We were finally able to stop her unpleasant experiences by giving her fifteen electroconvulsive treatments, in which electrodes are attached to the scalp, and the patient is given electrically induced seizures.

It is difficult for police to enforce the law that prohibits possession of LSD. The drug is a colorless, odorless, tasteless substance, often applied to the back of an envelope or a postage stamp or put into clothing; by licking the postage stamp or the envelope or chewing on the clothing, one can have an "experience." LSD is supplied in sugar cubes, capsules, tablets, liquid, or practically any other form. The most common format today is LSD-soaked paper known as blotter acid. Drops of LSD in a solution are put on paper with perforated squares that are artistically decorated. In some cases these decorations include Disney figures, Beavis and Butt-head, or Bart Simpson, to appeal to young children.[5]

The usual dose of LSD is between one hundred and two hundred micrograms. Black-market LSD has been analyzed and many times there are impurities present. LSD users do not know how much LSD they are purchasing. We have found a wide range of doses that were many times much less—and, in a few instances, much greater—than the dosage that was thought to be purchased. You can put enough LSD in an eye dropper to "turn on," or provide an LSD experience, to 10,000 people.

There was a great deal of interest about LSD in the 1960s in terms of its psychedelic, or "mind-expanding," properties. This interest led to a great deal of emphasis on psychedelic clothes, music, and art. Psychedelic clothes and art usually included intense colors. However, many people who participated in psychedelic art shows and psychedelic "happenings" did not use drugs.

LSD is erroneously called a mind-expanding drug, when really it is quite the opposite. The attention one can pay to the ordinary details of life is diminished after using LSD. The drug knocks out that part of the brain that has to do with filtering input. Consequently, a person who has taken LSD is aware of a multitude of stimulations, such as whispering, breathing, or people walking, that most of us filter out when we are paying conscious attention to some aspect of our surroundings. A person on a trip is also aware of intense internal stimulations, such as the hallucinations previously mentioned, internal fantasies, or dreamlike experiences. These internal stimulations make it equally difficult to pay conscious attention to what is really happening in the outside world.

## WHAT ARE THE PHYSICAL EFFECTS OF LSD?

There are few physical effects of LSD use. Dilated pupils is the most common. Sometimes people on an LSD trip wear sunglasses even at night to protect their dilated pupils from bright lights. There is also a transient chilliness, skin flushing, increase in blood pressure, increase in pulse rate, and increased respirations.

LSD is not physiologically addicting. This means that there are no withdrawal symptoms when one stops using it. The drug may be psychologically addicting, since a psychological need to keep using it may develop. There is no known lethal dose for humans, or known overdose. One tragic fatality occurred with a research elephant in Oklahoma. Here researchers calculated the dose of LSD on the elephant's massive body weight instead of its tiny brain weight. The elephant received a massive overdose of LSD, convulsed, and died.

There are two special points concerning the "freak trip," or adverse LSD reaction. First of all, it is impossible to predict who will have a bad experience. No psychiatric interviews, psychological testing, or stable life and job histories can screen out adverse reactors. I have seen people who are apparently normal have very severe reactions to LSD. Doctors, lawyers, other professionals, and people who seemed stable have become very disturbed after using LSD. Conversely, I have seen many people who are very disturbed and who had histories of severe emotional difficulties have no ill effects from using LSD. In other words, having no apparent emotional problems will not necessarily guarantee a good trip.

It is possible to have recurrences of the original symptoms up to three years after taking LSD, without using the drug again. There are various conditions that can stimulate a recurrence of the original trip. When some people are angry or upset, feel intensely about a personal problem, listen to certain kinds of music, or look at intense lights, they will have a recurrence. One young girl always had her recurrences on the freeway. She would be driving at night and rather than seeing one pair of headlights, she would see a thousand pairs of headlights and not know which were real. One man became frightened that a girlfriend would kill him during his original LSD trip. He no longer uses LSD. However, he has had a paranoid recurrence, and many times he has had the idea that his girlfriend is trying to hurt, or possibly kill him. He has been having these flashbacks for two years without using LSD again. Physicians use certain tranquilizers to reduce the anxiety and to diminish the frequency of the flashbacks experienced by some users. Some people report only a few flashbacks every month; nevertheless there have been some patients who have reported having fifteen to a hundred flashbacks per day.

Are there side effects in the LSD users in the community who never seek aid? Yes, and this has been one of the most interesting parts of our investigation. My associate and I attended "acid-head" parties at Big Sur, California, and gatherings around the beaches. We visited college students using LSD in Berkeley, California, and spent time in the Haight-Ashbury area in San Francisco. We found many LSD users who were disorganized, quite confused, and having flashbacks, but not seeking medical attention. We also found nonsuicidal deaths occurring after using LSD. Some deaths occur because the user experiences perceptual changes. One young girl leaped to a rocky beach thinking that the ocean had turned into a silk scarf. There were two young boys who felt they were having a religious experience and wanted to "become one" with several cars on Wilshire Boulevard. I had to restrain one young student who believed he had the power to fly and attempted to leap from a window in a Hollywood apartment. There are undoubtedly more accidental deaths never recorded or attributed directly to LSD.

What about set and setting? Set is one's attitude toward the LSD experience, and setting is the physical environment in which one takes LSD. Set and setting are important but not the only factors affecting the LSD trip. There is a great deal of mythology about LSD, including the idea that if you feel relaxed, take LSD with a friendly guide or a sitter, and have soft lighting, you won't have a bad trip. This is untrue; we have had many patients in our hospital who had all of these things going for them but still had bad trips.

**What are the long-term changes after using LSD?** Unlike many drugs, LSD does not require chronic use for one to have changes in one's attitude, personality, and motivation. We have seen some individuals manifest long-term changes

# ABOUT HALLUCINOGENS

Hallucinogenic drugs are substances that distort the perception of objective reality. The most well-known hallucinogens include phencyclidine, otherwise known as PCP, angel dust, or loveboat; lysergic acid diethylamide, commonly known as LSD or acid; mescaline and peyote; and psilocybin, or "magic" mushrooms. Under the influence of hallucinogens, the senses of direction, distance, and time become disoriented. These drugs can produce unpredictable, erratic, and violent behavior in users that sometimes leads to serious injuries and death. The effect of hallucinogens can last for 12 hours.

LSD produces tolerance, so that users who take the drug repeatedly must take higher and higher doses in order to achieve the same state of intoxication. This is extremely dangerous, given the unpredictability of the drug, and can result in increased risk of convulsions, coma, heart and lung failure, and even death.

Physical risks associated with using hallucinogens:
- increased heart rate and blood pressure
- sleeplessness and tremors
- lack of muscular coordination
- sparse, mangled, and incoherent speech
- decreased awareness of touch and pain that can result in self-inflicted injuries
- convulsions
- coma; heart and lung failure

Psychological risks associated with using hallucinogens:
- a sense of distance and estrangement
- depression, anxiety, and paranoia
- violent behavior
- confusion, suspicion, and loss of control
- flashbacks
- behavior similar to schizophrenic psychosis
- catatonic syndrome whereby the user becomes mute, lethargic, disoriented, and makes meaningless repetitive movements

Everyone reacts differently to hallucinogens—there's no way to predict if you can avoid a "bad trip."

after using LSD only once or twice. Many young people, after using LSD, have a dramatic change in their value systems. We have talked to high school students and college students who dropped out of school after using the drug. Professionals, businesspeople, and artists become much less interested in their former pursuits and more interested in mysticism, withdrawal, and preoccupation with the effects of LSD. When Timothy Leary, the famous "acid head" of the 1960s, said, "Turn on, tune in, drop out," he was describing an observable social phenomenon. We met a gentleman at a Hollywood Hills party who had spent months wandering around the desert near San Bernardino contemplating his LSD experience. Prior to using LSD he had been an international lawyer in New York City.

Another long-term change is a feeling of improvement but an objective loss of functioning. We have spoken with many people who felt they were more creative, that they had greater problem-solving ability, and that everything seemed less complicated after using LSD. Nevertheless, when we studied their lives closely we found they seemed to be doing much worse. We spoke with a mathematical engineer who maintained that after taking LSD he could do problems that normally required three to four hours in ten to fifteen minutes. Further questioning determined that he had lost his job. His reply to this fact was, "No one understands my answers anymore—but that's their problem." The perceptual distortions caused by LSD result in users having the feeling that they are doing better, while in reality they are doing much worse. LSD can give people the idea they are much stronger or have more powers than normal people. We spoke with one group who claimed to have extrasensory perception after using LSD. They felt they could read minds and "pick up vibrations" from other people. Our studies revealed that they did no better reading minds than if they would have merely guessed; however, they had the feeling that they were doing better.

Some people develop a missionary quality after using LSD. They are no longer content to take the drug themselves, but have the feeling that they should "turn on" everyone. We recently hospitalized a young mother who was giving her eighteen-month-old daughter LSD. One man became so enraptured with LSD that he took his life savings and purchased all the LSD he could, and marched up and down the beaches near Santa Monica passing out LSD to everyone he met—until he met a narcotics officer.

Another long-term effect of LSD seems to be that LSD users have difficulty tolerating feelings that occur in close relationships. "Love-ins" and "love sessions" were gatherings that we frequented for several months. We found that many young people, while talking about love, had a great deal of trouble communicating with others. This is reasonable, since LSD leaves the user with greater self-preoccupation and with less psychic energy available to care about another person. We found many LSD users describing their "love for humanity," "love for the world," and "love for nature"; however, they had a great deal of difficulty loving one other person.

**Why are so many young people attracted to LSD and hallucinogenic drugs?** Most of them are quite curious and concerned about who they are, what they are, and what is important in life. Many young people can be convinced the answer can be found in a capsule, a tablet, or a sugar cube. LSD and the other hallucinogenic drugs distort one's abilities to find real solutions to important problems. Young people are extremely concerned about their feelings. This is the time in life when a young person matures sexually, gets involved in all types of activities, and is very interested in society and the way it should be changed. Some young people with personality problems attempt to avoid their sexual and aggressive feelings by using LSD. The substance creates a drugged state or psychedelic effect that gives users the illusion that they have solved some of their emotional problems, when actually they have merely pushed them out of the way for a period of time. It is normal for young people to find different ways of accommodating their feelings, such as dating, political action, writing, or self-analysis. In a sense, LSD robs them of a chance to find solutions by creating the illusion that there are no more struggles. We talked to one user who said: "I don't have to hate anyone anymore, as long as I continue to use LSD and drugs." A young girl told us: "I am not interested in boys anymore and sex has no meaning after using LSD." The drug actually diminishes one's sexual and aggressive experiences.

**Should you turn on with LSD?** If you are in good health, not pregnant, and looking for a mind-altering experience, why not turn on, tune in, and drop out? There is no easy answer to this question. Young people must make this decision for themselves. It is difficult being a young person today. Society is far from perfect. Young people realize they have had adult heroes who often were models of drug abuse. It is sometimes difficult not to use drugs when one's friends maintain that this is the only way to "be in." Young people are curious, and most of us know that if someone really wants drugs they are available. Nevertheless, it is important to know the facts about LSD and other drugs. It is difficult to tell someone else what to do with his or her brain. I believe that if young people receive information about drugs, they are in a good position to make their own decisions. However, some people, because of serious psychological problems, are driven to using drugs as a defense against life and their feelings. But the majority of young people do have a choice. In a way, taking LSD is like playing Russian roulette. Some people use it with very few unpleasant experiences. Nevertheless, for some, LSD is a psychotic nightmare, and can mean several years in a mental hospital, flashbacks, and long-lasting personality changes.

It is unfortunate that there exists such a generation gap in our society today. Many adults discount anything that young people say. Similarly, some young people dismiss anyone over thirty as being "an old fogy" or "out of it." It is important to build bridges between the generations. One has only to take a look at the alcoholism, the suicide rate, and the social problems of today to realize that adults do not have all the answers.

## INHALANTS

A wide variety of chemical products that give off fumes are inhaled for their psychoactive effects. Many inhalants are chemicals that are found in household products, such as cleaning solvents and aerosols. Since the chemicals are cheap and easily available, this kind of drug abuse is popular with some kids as young as seven, many of whom are not aware that even one use can be deadly.

Several methods are used to bring inhalants into the body. "Sniffing" is breathing the chemical directly from the container. "Huffing" is soaking a rag or piece of clothing with a liquid or dissolved inhalant. Sometimes the cloth is stuffed into the mouth and sometimes the fumes are inhaled through the nose. "Bagging" means placing the inhalant in a plastic bag and inhaling it. The inhaled chemical and air in a plastic bag is breathed over and over again, so this is especially dangerous.

Most inhalants give the users an immediate high or rush, followed by a depressive effect. Ten-year-old Jon huffed paint thinner and other solvents occasionally over a period of six months. He felt better when using them than at any other time. One time after he huffed, his father thought he was drunk because his speech was slurred and he was confused. Another time, after Jon loaded his shirt collar with spot remover and breathed the fumes in school, he passed out. The school nurse called 911 and the medics who re-

# About Inhalants

Inhalants refer to substances that are sniffed or huffed to give the user an immediate head rush or high. They include a diverse group of chemicals that are found in consumer products such as aerosols and cleaning solvents. Inhalant use can cause a number of physical and emotional problems, and even one-time use can result in death.

Using inhalants even one time can put you at risk for:
- sudden death
- suffocation
- visual hallucinations and severe mood swings
- numbness and tingling of the hands and feet

Short-term effects of inhalants include:
- heart palpitations
- breathing difficulty
- dizziness
- headaches
- death

Prolonged use can result in:
- headache, muscle weakness, abdominal pain
- decrease or loss of sense of smell

- nausea and nosebleeds
- hepatitis
- violent behaviors
- irregular heartbeat
- liver, lung, and kidney impairment
- irreversible brain damage
- nervous system damage
- dangerous chemical imbalances in the body
- involuntary passing of urine and feces

Remember, using inhalants, even one time, can kill you. According to medical experts, death can occur in at least five ways:

1. asphyxia—solvent gases can significantly limit available oxygen in the air, causing breathing to stop
2. suffocation—typically seen with inhalant users who use bags
3. choking on vomit
4. careless behaviors in potentially dangerous settings
5. sudden sniffing death syndrome, presumably from cardiac arrest

sponded began treating him on the way to the hospital. Jon's teacher had noticed that he could not concentrate and now she knew why. The school counselor told Jon he was fortunate in having quick medical care that prevented permanent brain damage. This frightened him enough to stop using inhalants.

Using inhalants can cause a number of physical and emotional problems. Although sniffing and huffing do not get as much attention as other kinds of drug abuse, they are very risky. Death can occur in at least five ways: asphyxia because gases can significantly limit oxygen and cause breathing to stop; suffocation when users inhale in bags; choking on vomit; careless behaviors in potentially dangerous situations; and cardiac arrest.

# Uppers

## By Elizabeth Forsyth, M.D.

*Dr. Forsyth is a child psychiatrist and
the coauthor of fifteen books.*

**A**s their name suggests, uppers give the user a good feeling, or high. Two popular stimulant drugs, amphetamines and cocaine, are powerful uppers. Amphetamines are known on the street by many names, including speed, crank, pep pills, meth, and brain ticklers. Some slang terms for cocaine are coke, nose powder, crack, toke, and rock.

Jack, a recovering cocaine user, recalled that when he smoked crack he experienced an intense rush of pleasure, an ecstatic feeling that he was on top of the world, and a sense of well-being. He felt completely satiated and had no interest in food or sex while he was using drugs.

### WHAT HAPPENS IN THE BRAIN

Scientists have long known that cocaine, amphetamines, and other stimulants act on the brain's reward, or pleasure, center, but they have only recently begun to learn more about how these drugs work and why they make the user feel so good initially. The question of why people become addicted is complicated. Chemicals in the brain called neurotransmitters—especially one known as dopamine—are major factors in addiction. Addicting drugs—cocaine, amphetamines, heroin, alcohol, and nicotine—all raise the levels of dopamine in the brain. Some researchers suggest that dopamine is involved in dependence on substances, even chocolate and coffee. A rush of dopamine in your brain may even be responsible for the pleasure you feel when you experience anything you find enjoyable, from listening to music to eating candy. However, it would take about twenty-five pounds of chocolate for a person to feel high.[1]

The brain contains a network of about 100 billion cells called neurons, which send and receive messages. When a neuron is stimulated, it sends an electrical impulse through a thin, elongated projection of its cell body, called an axon. The axon does not touch the receiving parts, projections called dendrites, of the adjacent neuron. The gap between the nerve endings of the two neurons is called a synapse. Messages are transmitted across the synapse by means of neurotransmitters, which are stored at the nerve endings. These chemicals are released into the synapse between nerve cells and attach to receptor molecules on the dendrites of the receiving neuron, which then sends the electrical impulse along. Each receptor is designed to recognize only a certain neurotransmitter. After the message is transmitted, the neurotransmitter is reabsorbed by the sending cell to be used again, or it is broken down by one of many specialized enzymes.

## DOPAMINE AND MIND DRUGS

Dopamine is one of more than fifty known neurotransmitters. It is manufactured in nerve cells in certain parts of the brain. When these nerve cells are stimulated, dopamine is released into the synapse. Normally, it is then deactivated by an enzyme called monoamine oxidase (MAO), or it is reabsorbed.

When cocaine is introduced into the body, it disrupts the normal equilibrium of transmitters in the brain. Cocaine blocks the reabsorption of dopamine, so an excess amount accumulates at the synapse, flooding it with dopamine and triggering the rush. Amphetamines work in much the same way, causing an excess release of dopamine at the synapse.

In 1997, researchers at Brookhaven National Laboratory published a report that provided further evidence to support what other scientists have discovered about addiction. Cocaine addicts were given cocaine by vein, and then brain scans were performed to measure the activity of the system that governs the reabsorption of dopamine (dopamine transporter system, or DAT).[2] The researchers discovered that their subjects reported feeling high when at least 50 percent of the DAT molecules were blocked. The more transporter sites that were blocked by cocaine, the more intense the high.

Research done more than two decades ago linked addiction with dopamine. Cocaine-addicted rats in the laboratory kept themselves happy by pressing levers in their cages that dispensed cocaine. When they were injected with a drug that blocked the action of dopamine, they became frantic, pressing the levers endlessly in attempts to get more.

## FROM COCA LEAVES TO CRACK

Cocaine does have a legitimate medical use as a local anesthetic, and it is the only such compound that occurs naturally. The synthetic compounds that your dentist uses to numb your gums are chemically similar to cocaine.

Cocaine can be ingested by chewing the leaves or drinking the dissolved extract in a beverage, or it can be injected, snorted, or smoked. Before the 1970s, cocaine was very expensive, its use was rather limited, and its dangers were not fully recognized. But from 1976 to 1986, there was a fifteen-fold increase in the number of emergency room visits, deaths, and admissions to treatment facilities related to cocaine.[3] This increase was due mainly to the discovery of a new form of cocaine manufactured by illegal street chemists. This form is easy to concoct using readily available ingredients, and because it is relatively inexpensive, the street price dropped. Known as freebase or crack, it is a nearly pure form of the drug that is smoked; when inhaled, it is absorbed very rapidly through the lungs. Because it reaches the brain within five to eight seconds, crack acts almost instantly and gives the user an intense high that lasts just a few minutes.

## DRUG SCENE

At a crack house, a woman carries an infant with maggots crawling out of his diaper. A man "skin pops" his toddler with heroin to keep the child quiet while he enjoys his crack. Others are crouched in corners of the smoking room, smoking crack. Some are in various stages of paranoia and excitement, while some are having convulsions and seizures brought on by the crack use. Others are involved in sexual activity, fighting, and even stabbing and shooting each other over the price, quantity, or quality of the crack.

In contrast, the onset of cocaine's effects takes five to fifteen minutes when the leaves are chewed or when cocaine is swallowed in a drink. When it is sniffed, it is absorbed through the blood vessels in the nasal membranes and the time lag is about three minutes; injected into a vein, it acts in fifteen to thirty seconds.

*What Cocaine Can Do* In addition to raising dopamine levels, stimulants such as cocaine and amphetamines interfere with the normal balance of other neurotransmitters such as norepinephrine, causing an increase in the activity of the central nervous system. The user feels energized and more alert and restless. Appetite and the need for sleep diminish. Heart rate, blood pressure, and body temperature rise. When confronting a dangerous situation, the body behaves in the same way, pumping out adrenaline and causing the familiar "fight or flight" reaction. The difference is that using drugs overstimulates the nervous system artificially.

Although cocaine and other stimulants initially make people feel good, adverse reactions may occur, especially with continued use and larger doses. The person may become irritable, anxious, restless, and nervous. He or she may become agitated, angry, and aggressive, and may develop paranoid ideas—unwarranted suspicions that others want to harm them. Some users experience a condition known as formication, the sensation that insects are crawling under their skin.

Chronic users of cocaine may suffer severe or even fatal consequences due to stroke or heart attack. The drug constricts and weakens the vessels of the brain, causing bleeding, brain damage, seizures, or death. It also damages the heart muscle, which can cause disorders such as irregular rhythms, even in young people. The lungs may be affected when cocaine is smoked. A condition called "crack lung" causes pain, cough, fever, and shortness of breath. Contaminants in the cocaine may cause an allergic reaction in which the lungs fill with fluids and the individual may die from lack of oxygen.

Permanent mental problems, including poor judgment and inappropriate behavior, have been found to occur with long-term use and may be due to brain damage. In one survey, brain scans demonstrated shrinkage of the brain cortex in 50 percent of the chronic users who were studied.[4]

Some people have an exaggerated reaction to cocaine and overdose on small amounts. Chronic users become more sensitive to the toxic effects of the drug, and may experi-

Cocaine is a white powder that comes from the leaves of the South American coca plant. Cocaine is either "snorted" through the nasal passages or injected intravenously. Cocaine belongs to a class of drugs known as stimulants, which tend to give a temporary illusion of limitless power and energy that leave the user feeling depressed, edgy, and craving more. Crack is a smokable form of cocaine that has been chemically altered. Cocaine and crack are highly addictive. This addiction can erode physical and mental health and can become so strong that these drugs dominate all aspects of an addict's life.

Physical risks associated with using cocaine and crack:
- increases in blood pressure, heart rate, breathing rate, and body temperature
- heart attacks, strokes, and respiratory failure
- hepatitis or AIDS through shared needles
- brain seizures
- reduction of the ability to resist and combat infection

Psychological risks:
- violent, erratic, or paranoid behavior
- hallucinations and "coke bugs"—a sensation of imaginary insects crawling over the skin
- confusion, anxiety, and depression, loss of interest in food or sex
- "cocaine psychosis"—losing touch with reality, loss of interest in friends, family, sports, hobbies, and other activities

Some users spend hundreds or thousands of dollars on cocaine and crack each week and will do anything to support their habit. Many turn to drug selling, prostitution, or other crimes.

Cocaine and crack use has been a contributing factor in a number of drownings, car crashes, falls, burns, and suicides.

Cocaine and crack addicts often become unable to function sexually. Even first-time users may experience seizures or heart attacks, which can be fatal.

ence serious problems after taking their accustomed dose. Seizures, elevated blood pressure, respiratory depression, coma, and death can follow.

Chronic users suffer other health problems. They are often malnourished because these drugs decrease the appetite. When they inject drugs of any kind, they are subject to the risk of infection from HIV (the virus that causes AIDS), hepatitis, and other diseases.

Although there are some users who take cocaine occasionally and never increase their use of the drug, many others become hooked. They go on binges called runs, during which they inject, snort, or smoke cocaine sometimes as frequently as every ten minutes in order to stay on a constant high, using up tremendous amounts of energy.

*Crashing* The body metabolizes (breaks down) cocaine very rapidly, so the high disappears suddenly. Then the user experiences a crash—feelings of depression that may last for hours, days, or weeks. One addict told a typical story of going without sleep for four or five days at a time, eating almost nothing, until he was exhausted or used up all his drugs. Then he would crash; he became terribly depressed, felt like dying, and experienced tremendous fatigue and insatiable hunger. After a day of sleep, the cycle would begin again.

Many cocaine addicts use downers to come off a high in order to avoid crashing. They often use drugs such as alcohol, Valium, or heroin, creating a vicious cycle and becoming dependent on the second drug.

Withdrawal from cocaine or amphetamines is another problem. It is not the same as crashing, although the symptoms are similar. After going through a binge and crash cycle, an abuser may start feeling better after a few days and may believe that he or she is not really dependent on the drug. But within weeks, withdrawal symptoms set in: mental depression, fatigue, lack of energy, and absence of motivation, along with an intense craving for the drug that is nearly impossible to resist unless the user is in treatment. Remaining in the environment associated with drug use is dangerous because the user is surrounded by cues that trigger the craving. One former user related that for months after quitting, the sight of bare arms revived an almost irresistible urge for drugs again.[5] Many people are not aware that withdrawal symptoms can last for at least several months, and that the danger for relapse remains high, especially if treatment is discontinued too soon.

## AMPHETAMINES

Benzedrine was the first amphetamine to be marketed. During the 1930s it was used in inhalers as a nasal decongestant, and in tablet and injectable forms for treatment of depression, narcolepsy (a condition characterized by sudden spells of sleep during the day), and a few other disorders. However, benzedrine and other amphetamines soon became popular for their fatigue-fighting effects among students, truck drivers, and others who needed to stay awake for long periods. In the 1950s and 1960s, they were manufactured in huge quantities with no controls by the Food and Drug Administration, and were widely used for their stimulant and appetite-suppressing effects. In 1962, an estimated 8 billion amphetamine tablets were produced worldwide.[6] Many people began abusing these drugs, which were easily available at that time. After the federal government tightened regulations in 1970, the drugs were manufactured and bought illegally.

*Meth* There are many street versions of speed, but methamphetamine, or "meth," is the current favorite. It is cheaper than cocaine and the high lasts longer. In the 1990s, a new and potent smokable form known as ice was developed illegally. Smoking ice results in a rapid and intense high, its effects last longer than those of crack cocaine, and it results

Methamphetamine is a stimulant drug chemically related to amphetamine but with stronger effects on the central nervous system. Street names for the drug include "speed," "meth," and "crank."

Methamphetamine is used in pill form, or in powdered form by snorting or injecting. Crystallized methamphetamine—known as "ice," "crystal," or "glass"—is a smokable and more powerful form of the drug.

The effects of methamphetamine use include:
- increased heart rate and blood pressure
- increased wakefulness; insomnia
- increased physical activity
- decreased appetite
- respiratory problems
- extreme anorexia
- hyperthermia, convulsions, and cardiovascular problems, which can lead to death
- euphoria
- irritability
- confusion
- tremors
- anxiety, paranoia, or violent behavior
- possible irreversible damage to blood vessels in the brain, producing strokes

Methamphetamine users who inject the drug and share needles are at risk for acquiring HIV/AIDS.

Methamphetamine is an increasingly popular drug at raves (all night dancing parties), and as part of a number of drugs used by college-age students.

Marijuana and alcohol are commonly listed as additional drugs of abuse among methamphetamine treatment admissions.

Most of the methamphetamine-related deaths (92%) reported in 1994 involved methamphetamine in combination with at least one other drug, most often alcohol (30%), heroin (23%), or cocaine (21%).

Researchers continue to study the long-term effects of methamphetamine use.

in a higher incidence of overdoses and bad side effects, such as hallucinations and disturbed behavior and speech.[7]

Today's meth (crystal, crank, speed) is as addictive as crack, with highs that can last as long as eight hours. Users tend to be white, blue-collar males. Meth production is believed to be one of the fastest-growing cottage industries in the Midwest.

There is great concern about the huge increase in the use of meth in the 1990s and the proliferation of illicit labs for its production. In addition, a large amount of the supply is smuggled into this country from Mexico. Since meth can be made inexpensively and easily using ordinary chemicals, it has become widely available. The average age of first use has dropped, and ten- to thirteen-year-olds are using meth. In some places, it has surpassed marijuana as the preferred drug among high school kids.

---

**DRUG SCENE: METH**
Raina and her friend went to a popular place for parties along the Eel River in Potter Valley, where they tried methamphetamine that was supplied by a drug dealer. The girls became disoriented, were sexually assaulted, and left the party in a confused state. What happened after that is a mystery, except for the fact that Raina drowned in the river.

---

The illicit labs present other hazards. The chemicals are flammable and have caused fires and explosions. Fumes killed a three-year-old boy whose parents were manufacturing meth in their apartment.[8] Residues left behind or secretly dumped in landfills or waterways are toxic, and some cause cancer.[9]

The effects of amphetamines and cocaine on the body and on mood are similar. They usually produce an initial rush of euphoria, along with increased wakefulness and energy, feelings of confidence, and increased ability to concentrate. Some athletes take amphetamines because they believe their performance will improve. Amphetamines can ward off feelings of fatigue and temporarily increase stamina, but they have little actual affect on performance.

As with cocaine, users go on binges, or runs, and then crash. During these high periods, they may become extremely hyperactive, cleaning house or painting walls nonstop. One woman vacuumed her apartment, then dumped the dirt back on the floor and vacuumed again.

Tolerance to the mood-altering effects and psychological dependency develop as with cocaine, and symptoms of withdrawal appear when the drug is stopped. Laboratory animals who have learned to self-administer amphetamines have been observed to choose drugs instead of food and water; they die from exhaustion in their frantic efforts to feed their high.[10]

Prolonged use or high doses of amphetamines can result in a psychotic reaction, with disturbed thinking, paranoia, depression, and violent, homicidal, or suicidal behavior. Although the mental symptoms usually disappear within a week after stopping the drug, some users are left with permanent mental problems.

## RITALIN

Methylphenidate, a compound that is chemically related to amphetamines and better known by its trade name, Ritalin, is one of the most commonly prescribed stimulant drugs. It is often used to treat children with a condition known as attention deficit/hyperactivity disorder. This disorder causes overly active behavior, restlessness, impulsivity, short attention span, and difficulty in concentrating. Although it might not seem logical to give a stimulant to a hyperactive individual, oddly enough Ritalin works to reduce these symptoms. Ritalin is a useful drug when used appropriately under medical supervision. Although it is sometimes abused, some researchers think that it is less likely to be abused than cocaine because its effects last longer. They found that both drugs give pleasure mainly while the concentration of dopamine in the brain is rising, which occurs during the first few minutes. When the concentration levels off, the brain begins to adapt, and the pleasurable feelings are lost. Cocaine disappears so rapidly that the brain does not have time to adapt, and is ready to respond again in a short time. In contrast, Ritalin remains in the brain for several hours, and it prevents the brain from reacting to a new dose during that time.

## DIET PILLS

Diet pills are very popular because so many people want to lose weight. Amphetaminelike compounds such as Redux and Preludin that have stimulant and appetite-suppressant effects do cause weight loss in the first few months of use, but most people gain back all the weight they lose. Although these pills have a lower potential for abuse than other stimulants, users can develop tolerance and dependence. A popular combination of diet drugs known as "fen-phen" was taken off the market in 1997 because the pills caused serious heart and lung damage in some people.

In addition to cocaine, there are numerous other plant stimulants. Caffeine and nicotine are probably the best known of these naturally occurring substances; some of these naturally occurring substances are discussed in chapter 7.

# Downers

*Elizabeth Forsyth, M.D. and*
*Margaret O. Hyde*

**W**hat do pink ladies, dillies, and green weenies have in common? You won't find them on any restaurant menu, but you might find them being sold illegally on the street. Popularly known as downers, they are mind-altering compounds that act by slowing down the functioning of the brain and central nervous system. These drugs are called depressants, not because they make you depressed or blue, but because they depress or inhibit the firing of nerve cells in the brain and central nervous system. Downers have a number of legitimate medical uses: to induce sleep, relieve anxiety, relax muscles, and control epileptic seizures. In higher doses, most can produce general anesthesia, and in excessive amounts, they can result in coma and death.

Depressants include four main categories: sedative-hypnotics; a group of various over-the-counter (nonprescription) sedatives, antihistamines, and muscle relaxants; alcohol; and the opioids (narcotic drugs that have opium or morphinelike properties). See chapter 7 for a discussion of alcohol.

## BARBITURATES AND OTHER SEDATIVE-HYPNOTICS

Until the middle of the nineteenth century, the only sleeping medicines available were various unpredictable and unreliable potions, herbal concoctions, alcoholic beverages, and laudanum (an opium derivative). But since the beginning of the twentieth century, many more reliable and effective sleeping medications and sedatives have been developed.

In the United States today, more than 150 million prescriptions are written for sedative-hypnotic medications every year.[1] (Hypnotic used in this sense means sleep-inducing and has nothing to do with the psychological state known as a hypnotic trance.) Most of these drugs fall into two groups: the benzodiazepines and the barbiturates.

The sedatives or tranquilizers have a calming effect, while the hypnotics produce drowsiness and sleep. Sometimes referred to as solid alcohol, the sedative-hypnotics have an effect similar to that of alcohol. If you take a sleeping pill or sedative, in addition to making you drowsy, it affects your breathing, slows your reflexes, impairs muscular coordination, and lowers your inhibitions. Like alcohol, these drugs can impair your thinking, memory, and judgment.

The first drug in the barbiturate group was introduced in the early 1900s. Soon more than 2,500 types were synthesized, with about 50 available for medical use. These drugs were welcomed because they were found to relieve insomnia and anxiety and control epileptic seizures, so physicians prescribed them by the millions.

In the 1940s, their potential for abuse was recognized, and states began passing laws against nonprescription barbiturates. Despite their known dangers, even when taken as prescribed, they remained the most popular downers until about 1961, when the first of the Valium-type drugs—the benzodiazepines—was introduced.[2] Long-acting barbiturates, such as phenobarbital, are used mostly for controlling seizures, and sometimes for sedation. They take effect slowly and last for about twenty-four hours. Ultrafast-acting barbiturates such as sodium pentothal are used for anesthesia. When injected into the bloodstream, they produce unconsciousness within minutes. Neither of these types holds much attraction for abusers.

**Abuse, Tolerance, and Overdose** The compounds most likely to be abused are the intermediate or shorter-acting barbiturates used as sleeping pills, such as Seconal (red devils), Amytal (blue dolls), Nembutal (yellow jackets), and Tuinal (rainbows, double trouble). These drugs act in about thirty minutes and are the most like alcohol in their effects. Taken as sleeping pills in the prescribed amount at bedtime, they produce sleep. But when they are used in social settings, often in larger doses and sometimes together with alcohol, they make people feel euphoric, relaxed, and less inhibited. Sometimes users become agitated and combative instead of relaxed, depending on the circumstances. They may look and act drunk, slurring their speech and staggering about. They also suffer the same kind of hangover that alcohol abusers experience the next day.

If physicians prescribe these drugs so widely and if they have legitimate medical uses, you might think they are safe to use occasionally without a medical purpose. But there are serious problems associated with their use.

One such danger is overdosing. Overdosing causes cold and clammy skin, shallow breathing, weak and rapid pulse, lowered blood pressure, coma, and eventual respiratory failure and death if the person does not receive treatment. This can happen when sedative-hypnotic drugs are used with alcohol or other drugs, as is often the case. The combination of sedative-hypnotics with other depressants or with certain drugs used for treating serious mental illness has an additive effect, and in some cases, a synergistic effect. (Synergistic means that the drugs enhance or increase each other's effect. Here, two plus two equals more than four.) The result is a greater depression of the respiratory center in the brain and an increased likelihood of death. Many teenagers have never heard of synergy and are ignorant of this particular risk.

The sedative-hypnotics, often combined with other drugs, are frequently responsible for many accidental and intentional suicides. When their thinking and judgment are impaired, many users forget how many pills they have taken. Overdosing sometimes occurs when users keep popping pills quickly without waiting long enough for the full effect of the drug.

Your body quickly develops physical tolerance to drugs, especially to the barbiturates. Physical tolerance occurs when the liver cells become increasingly efficient at breaking down the drug. This means the user must take more in order to obtain the same psychological effect once received with lower doses. The body becomes so accustomed to the drug that larger doses are needed just to feel normal. The danger point is reached when a chronic user needs a dose close to the level that would be lethal. At this stage, a mistake or confusion about dose may result in a fatal overdose.

Physical dependence on barbiturates can develop within a month of use, and it is extremely dangerous because of the very serious and sometimes fatal withdrawal reactions— reactions that are worse than those of morphine or heroin withdrawal. Medical supervision is necessary because suddenly stopping or rapidly decreasing the dose can result in symptoms that include delirium and severe convulsions, sometimes beginning within hours of the last dose.

If a pregnant woman takes sedatives, her baby is more likely to be born with defects such as cleft palate. Because the drug reaches the baby from the mother's bloodstream via the placenta, the baby may suffer withdrawal symptoms at birth.

## BZDs

The benzodiazepines (sometimes abbreviated BZDs) have replaced the barbiturates and other downers to a great extent. The BZDs act on the neurotransmitter gamma aminobutyrate (GABA) to produce a calming effect. They also affect dopamine and serotonin, targeting receptors in the limbic system, the brain center concerned with emotions. They turn on the body's own "feel-good" chemicals. They are better sleeping medications than the barbiturates because they produce more normal sleep, interfering very little with REM (dreaming) sleep. Triazolam, better known by its trade name of Halcion, is a very short-acting sleeping pill that is broken down rapidly and has less hangover effect than other drugs.

The BZDs are also safer than the barbiturates because there is a large difference between the amount needed for sedation and the amount that would cause an overdose. Studies have shown that the rate of drug overdose decreased after the use of barbiturates began to decline and the BZDs were substituted.[3]

Despite early enthusiasm for these supposedly safe new drugs, there are some serious problems. Many users are under the impression that you can't overdose on BZDs, but this isn't true. These drugs have only a slight effect on respiration when used alone, but because they don't produce as much of a rush or euphoria as barbiturates, abusers often take them with other drugs.

Central nervous system depression is multiplied when BZDs are taken with other downers; interaction with alcohol can be lethal, even after only a few pills and a couple of drinks. The drugs last for a very long time in the body tissues, and people may not be aware that even a short-acting sleeping pill such as Halcion can have aftereffects the next day. Longer-acting BZDs can last for several days.

BZDs, like other depressants, cause decreased mental alertness and impaired physical coordination. One source reports that 10 percent of drivers arrested for DUI were found to have alcohol and sedatives in their blood.[4]

As with the barbiturates, development of tolerance is another problem. This means that the user must take more and more of the drug to get the same psychological effects. Physical addiction occurs more easily than experts believed when the BZDs were introduced, even when low doses are taken as prescribed for a year.

More people have died withdrawing from Valium than from overdosing on it.[5] Because the BZDs remain in the body for so long, withdrawal symptoms can last for several months, coming and going in cycles, and may include severe anxiety, insomnia, difficulty concentrating, and—less frequently—seizures or hallucinations. Another problem is that withdrawal symptoms can be mistaken for a return of the condition (such as anxiety or insomnia) for which the drug was prescribed in the first place. This may lead to increasing the dosage to get rid of the symptoms.

In a small number of cases, BZDs have been associated with unusual reactions such as violent behavior and amnesia. The sedative called flunitrazepam, or Rohypnol (its trade name), is popular in rave clubs, in which all-night underground parties are held. It gained notoriety as the "date rape drug" because of reports that young women were sexually assaulted after experiencing its effects. These effects include sedation and lessening of inhibitions with later difficulty in remembering the event. The drug is not available in the United States, but it is often smuggled into the country from Mexico and Colombia.[6]

It has been estimated that at least 25 percent of people taking benzodiazepines do not take them as prescribed, exceed the prescribed dose, or obtain them illegally.[7] BZBs are also at times not prescribed correctly. According to one survey, one third of a group of patients on prescribed BZDs had serious depression and should have been taking antidepressant medication instead.[8]

## LUDES AND GHB

A number of sedative-hypnotics used in the past few decades have fallen into disfavor or have been withdrawn from the legitimate market because of their adverse effects and their potential for abuse. The following are a few of these.

---

### DRUG SCENE: GHB

Four boys go into a kitchen late at night with supplies to make a drug known as GHB. They have read that the drug acts as an aphrodisiac, induces sleep, provides a hangover-free high, and builds muscles. The boys, who found the recipe for GHB in an underground book about steroids, had no problem purchasing the ingredients; they are all legal.

The boys mix the lye and the other ingredients according to the recipe, and they cook the concoction as instructed. They can hardly wait until the cooking process is finished so they can begin their new muscle-building program. In fact, they do not wait long enough, and the lye in the mixture is still strong. One boy goes into convulsions and falls into the supply of lye, causing severe burns to his arms and forehead. He is taken to the hospital. The other boys are not seriously hurt, but their dreams of looking "cut" by taking GHB will not materialize.

---

Methaqualone, more well-known by its trade name Quaaludes or its street name "ludes," was considered (as were other nonbarbiturate sedatives) to be nonaddictive and was widely prescribed as sleeping medication. Called the "love drug"[9] because it acts as an aphrodisiac, it was removed from the market in the 1980s because of heavy abuse.[10] This prompted a huge illegal business importing and producing methaqualone. Sometimes it is combined with antihistamines or with other drugs to enhance its sedative and pleasurable effects. The illicit street versions of ludes are more dangerous than the original prescription Quaaludes because they contain varying and unknown combinations of methaqualone and other drugs.

Gamma hydroxybutyrate, or GHB, is a sedative-hypnotic used as a sleeping medication in the 1960s and 1970s. In the 1990s, bodybuilders began using it because of its effects on muscle. GHB (also called "grievous bodily harm") has become one of the drugs popular in rave clubs. Although it was taken off the market because of adverse side effects such as respiratory depression and seizures, illegal versions are sold on the street.[11]

Chloral hydrate was widely used as a sleeping medication and anticonvulsant before other drugs became available, but it is not prescribed very often now.[12] Abusers sometimes combine it with alcohol, thus increasing the depressant effect and resulting in a potentially dangerous knockout potion known as a Mickey Finn.

## HEROIN AND OTHER NARCOTICS

Narcotics (opiates and opioids) are natural, semisynthetic, and synthetic derivatives of the opium poppy. Drugs such as morphine, codeine, heroin, methadone, Darvon, and Percodan fall into this category. They are all depressants, but they are also potent painkillers, and except for heroin (which is illegal) they are prescribed to relieve pain and to control coughing and diarrhea. But because of their pleasurable effects and addictive properties, they can cause problems when taken for nonmedical reasons. Most nonmedical users take these drugs to experience euphoria, to avoid pain, and to relieve withdrawal symptoms.[13]

Heroin's declining prices and the lack of knowledge about the devastation it causes have led to a recent increase in its use. The availability of cheaper, smokable heroin encouraged many young people to experiment.

New users frequently began by smoking or snorting, but many progress to injecting, the more efficient way of using the drug. But injecting heroin has its dangers. Tremendous variation in the strength of street heroin raises the chances of overdose, and impurities plus bacteria or viruses in the heroin can cause illness. The use of contaminated needles increases the chances of getting HIV, the virus that causes AIDS. Fifty to 80 percent of heroin addicts in New York City who use needles are HIV positive.[14]

A current trend in some areas of the country is "chasing the dragon." When heroin in the form of powder or a resin known as tar is heated on a piece of aluminum foil, it liquefies and then evaporates. Users inhale the smoke, which conjures up images of a dragon as it rises and curls.

An underground fashion of dragons on baseball caps and shirts developed into "heroin chic" in the 1990s. Drug glorification was part of the fashion scene for the first half of the decade.[15] Models with a wan, bedraggled look, carefully made-up and posed to look like strung-out drug addicts, were part of a movement that romanticized heroin. On February 4, 1997, a prestigious photographer named Davide Sorrenti overdosed on heroin. His drug-related death played a major part in the trend away from "heroin chic" to more upbeat photos of models.

Music has carried messages about drugs for many years, and continues to do so. But in the wake of the death of a number of rockers from heroin overdoses, some musicians joined the fight against drugs. For example, MusiCares is dedicated to attacking drug problems in the music industry and providing access to rehabilitation for musicians.

Heroin's threat as an emerging drug is a matter of great concern. Is it going to unfold like the crack epidemic? Cocaine and opiate waves have succeeded one another since 1885, and each drug cycle carried with it the seed of its own destruction. Experts predict the new heroin wave won't be as alarming as the one in the 1970s because people are much better informed about drugs now. No one denies that heroin can produce an unbelievable high for a short time, but despite drug education initiatives, many of the new users do not hear about the dead-end consequences of the drug or listen to those who warn, "It's so good, don't even try it once."

Shannon said she first snorted heroin a year ago in San Francisco. She moved from San Francisco to New York to get rid of her habit, but it followed her. Soon she wasn't getting high enough by snorting or smoking heroin, so she tried injecting it. She told herself this would only be a temporary thing until she was used to her new job as an administrative assistant. She got to the point where she wasn't doing heroin to feel good anymore; she needed it just to get to work in the morning. Shannon lost weight. She didn't look well. Her eyes were swollen and her skin was gray under her makeup. She knew she had arrived at a new status. She was a drug addict.

One day, Shannon saw a picture of woman with the caption, "I saw a dog and thought if I was a dog I wouldn't be addicted to heroin. I wish I was a dog." She managed to find a slot in a methadone clinic, where she took a dose of methadone daily to keep the heroin craving away and was able to enjoy life again. Unfortunately, there are not nearly enough openings in treatment centers for all the heroin addicts who want to be free again.

Heroin is not used medically today and has no legitimate use as a relaxant because of its dangerous addicting potential.

There is no magic pill that can solve problems or make people happy, but many other drugs are available that can reduce stress and anxiety and that are safe when taken under a doctor's supervision. They are not for everybody and are easily misused. Users buy illicit street drugs or they forge, steal, or buy prescriptions. They often go to many different physicians for a variety of medical conditions and obtain a prescription from each one, thus enabling them to satisfy their need for higher than normal doses.

State laws concerning the prescribing of sedative-hypnotic drugs have been made more stringent, and health care professionals are becoming more aware of the potential risks of the indiscriminate use of downers.

# The Marijuana Controversy

*Margaret O. Hyde*

**M**arijuana is believed to be the second most popular intoxicant in the United States today, with alcohol being the first. Marijuana is a subtle drug that is the subject of many myths and controversies. About 10 million people smoke it as a cigarette (called a joint or a nail) or in a pipe (or a bong) on a monthly basis.[1] Marijuana is also smoked in cigars, known as blunts.

Contrary to popular belief, most teenagers do not smoke marijuana. Studies show that in 1996, about 34 percent of tenth graders and 36 percent of high school seniors used marijuana. Although use by high school students increased after a decade of decline, marijuana use by twelve- to seventeen-year-olds dropped in 1996.[2] "Everyone does it," is a saying that does not apply.

**A BRIEF HISTORY OF POT**
Many ideas about marijuana have changed and continue to change. In 1936, a film called *Reefer Madness* was produced

as an attempt to scare young people away from trying the drug. In 1937, Narcotics Commissioner Harry J. Anslinger denounced marijuana as an "Assassin of Youth"[3] in a magazine article in which he described it as being as dangerous as a coiled rattlesnake. He cited a case in which it was claimed that a whole family was murdered by a young marijuana addict. Narcotics officers conjured up blatant scare stories of marijuana smokers prowling the streets with butcher knives in hand, searching for women to rape. Women who smoked marijuana were portrayed as being so addicted that they left home to become prostitutes for their suppliers.[4] An antimarijuana campaign by newspapers published by W. R. Hearst played a part in the banning of marijuana, even for medicinal uses.[5]

Through the years, young people laughed at the 1936 film *Reefer Madness*, knowing that marijuana was not the wildly dangerous drug that the film portrayed. Scare tactics are credited with laying the foundation for the widespread use of marijuana by rebellious youth during the next few decades.[6]

The strength of marijuana has changed through the years. New breeding and cultivation techniques have raised the level of THC (delta-9-tetrahydrocannabinol), the chemical that triggers the most powerful effects on people. The average content of THC twenty years ago was 0.4 percent; a few varieties today may contain as much as 10 percent.[7] Some marijuana grown indoors that was seized in raids tested up to 14 percent, but these "boutique strains" are expensive and not available to the average user.

## IMMEDIATE EFFECTS

The immediate effects of marijuana are often subtle. Reactions vary from almost none to panic. Most users feel relaxed, but the mental effects are very dependent on the setting in which the drug is used and the personality of the user. In rare cases, marijuana smokers have disturbing reactions of anxiety that may be accompanied by paranoid thoughts. The smoker may become fearful of dying or going mad, and may even panic. These reactions occur most frequently in inexperienced users. Flashbacks may occur in psychedelic drug users, and some reports say they may occur without previous use of these drugs. Smokers may experience a psychotic reaction to marijuana if they are vulnerable to psychosis under any stress, a change in either consciousness or body image.[8]

David's reactions to pot are rather typical. After a period of feeling relaxed, he grows very hungry. He eats a slice of pizza, and decides it is the best pizza he has ever tasted. Of course, it is just like the slice he ate earlier in the day, but his perception of it has changed. He listens to a CD and the THC that has been absorbed into the fatty tissue of his brain makes the music seem the best he has ever heard. His hearing has not changed, but his perception of the music is different.

David feels wonderful as his friend Caitlin massages his back. This is something he always enjoys, but now the feeling is much better. Pot has altered his perception of this and numerous other messages that come from his environment.

When David is smoking marijuana, his world seems wonderful. He is not concerned about the paper that is due tomorrow, the money he owes Fred (even though Fred is sitting on the same sofa), the fender he bent on the car last week. He is living in a different world, or, at least, one that seems different. When the effects of the marijuana wear off, his problems will still be there.

David likes forgetting his problems, so he smokes every day. He doesn't notice that his habit has become an important part of his life. He says that he can stop smoking any time he wants to, but he hasn't wanted to for months. He thinks he is enjoying the "real thing," only it isn't real.

# ABOUT MARIJUANA

Marijuana is the most widely used illicit drug in the United States and tends to be the first illegal drug teens use.

The physical effects of marijuana use, particularly on developing adolescents, can be acute.

Short-term effects of using marijuana:

- sleepiness
- difficulty keeping track of time
- impaired or reduced short-term memory
- reduced ability to perform tasks requiring concentration and coordination, such as driving a car
- increased heart rate
- potential cardiac dangers for those with preexisting heart disease
- bloodshot eyes
- dry mouth and throat
- decreased social inhibitions
- paranoia and hallucinations

Long-term effects of using marijuana:

- enhanced risk of bronchitis, emphysema, and cancer
- decrease in testosterone levels for men; also lower sperm counts and difficulty having children
- increase in testosterone levels for women; also increased risk of infertility
- diminished or extinguished sexual pleasure
- psychological dependence requiring more of the drug to get the same effect
- depression
- tremors
- irritability

Marijuana blocks the messages going to your brain and alters your perceptions and emotions, vision, hearing, and coordination.

A recent study of 1,023 trauma patients admitted to a shock trauma unit found that one third had marijuana in their blood.

## MARIJUANA LONG-TERM

Long-term, regular marijuana smoking has adverse effects, but these were not immediately apparent to its users when the drug became popular in the 1950s and 1960s.[9] Since there is not a rapid onset of withdrawal, many smokers deny that it occurs. THC is retained in the fat cells of the body, and withdrawal takes place only after a period of abstinence of from several weeks to a month after a person stops.[10]

Louis smoked for five years before deciding to quit. Then he stopped for a week and he felt great. He did not recognize the withdrawal symptoms of depression, sleep disturbance, irritability, slight tremors, and other withdrawal effects that appeared a month after he stopped. He did not recognize the craving that made him start again as a withdrawal symptom.[11]

Although the major effects of marijuana smoking last only about four to six hours, residual amounts can disrupt some physiological, mental, and emotional functions for a longer period. Urine tests may be positive for as long as ten to fifteen days in daily users and as long as a year in heavy users. Even casual use may result in positive tests for about five to seven days.[12]

While the effects of marijuana on health are still being debated, a number of facts seem clear. The effects of marijuana differ from individual to individual. Regularly observed physical effects include a substantial increase in the heart rate, bloodshot eyes, dry mouth and throat, and increased appetite. Short-term memory is reduced, but ideas flow rapidly and the smoker may feel high or hilarious. The most common response is a calm, mildly euphoric state in which time seems to slow down. A song on a compact disc that lasts about two minutes may seem to take twenty minutes. Sensitivity to touch, sights, and sound are enhanced, so the words of the song that once seemed jumbled are now clear—or at least, they seem clear.

Reaction time slows and coordination and attention are impaired. The distorted sense of time mentioned above applies to any physical or mental activity, including driving a car. A smoker driving down the highway at thirty-five miles per hour might feel as if the car were moving at a hundred miles per hour. Or when driving at a hundred miles per hour, a smoker might feel that the speed was twenty-five.[13] These reactions make driving a car or operating complex machinery while under the influence of marijuana dangerous. Some impairment persists for at least several hours after the feeling of intoxication has passed.

Another major risk of marijuana smoking is respiratory disease. Long-term heavy marijuana use affects the lungs, much as nicotine does, and causes the same diseases: bronchitis, emphysema, and lung cancer.[14] The damage from a few joints has been compared to a whole pack of cigarettes because the smoke is held in the lungs longer and tar content is higher. Smoking both marijuana and tobacco does much more damage to the air passages and lungs than smoking only one of those drugs.[15]

There are clinical reports of "amotivational syndrome" with heavy use of marijuana. Its symptoms are apathy, aimlessness, passivity, and lack of ambition. Many people who smoke marijuana heavily lose interest in goals and future plans. They like being high, and seem to be satisfied to watch their own lives and the world go by. Some experts claim this syndrome is due to hormone changes, brain damage, sedation, and/or depression. Since this syndrome is not evident in Greek or Caribbean farm laborers, who are heavy marijuana users, it has been suggested that it affects only those people whose employment requires more complex thinking.[16]

Marijuana can make kids mess up in school, in sports or clubs, and with friends. According to the United States Department of Health and Human Services Monitoring the Future survey, marijuana has been shown to damage motivation and interest in one's goals and activities.[17]

There is also a strong link between marijuana, unsafe sex, and the spread of HIV, the virus that causes AIDS.[18] Because marijuana lowers inhibitions, many people who would not have sex without a condom or become involved in sexual relations are exposed to the virus.

## IS MARIJUANA ADDICTING?

There is less controversy in recent years about whether or not marijuana is addicting. If addiction is defined by compulsive, repeated use in spite of adverse circumstances, marijuana is addictive. An estimated 100,000 Americans turn to rehabilitation centers each year for help in overcoming marijuana habits.[19]

Certainly, there are smokers who begin in the morning and continue all day. For them, marijuana use is compulsive and uncontrolled, a major feature of their daily life. Unfortunately, many teenage marijuana smokers do not recognize that their use of this drug is changing their behavior.

Dr. Mark Gold, an expert in the field of drug abuse, believes there is some sort of genetic vulnerability to marijuana use, but this predisposition is not detected until after the smoker has begun using. And when the smokers do continue despite the consequences, they deny the problem. Denial is a characteristic common to all marijuana addicts.[20]

## IS MARIJUANA A GATEWAY DRUG?

The "stepping stone hypothesis" is another area in which there is controversy. Many authorities state that marijuana is a gateway drug, one that leads to the use of other illegal drugs. According to the Harvard Medical School report on addiction, almost anyone who uses any illegal drugs smoked marijuana first, just as almost anyone who smokes marijuana has drunk alcohol first. Most alcohol users do not smoke marijuana. Most marijuana smokers do not move on to heroin or cocaine, even though most heroin and cocaine users smoked marijuana first. People who use drugs are somewhat more likely to find themselves in the company of other illegal drug users and this may be an important factor in their progression to drugs like heroin, cocaine, and speed.[21]

However, a hypothesis published in the journal *Science* in 1997 provides strong support for the gateway theory. New findings, based on studies with rats, indicate that changes in the brain chemistry from marijuana are identical to changes in the brains of people who abuse heroin, nicotine, alcohol, and cocaine. These findings support the idea that chronic marijuana use may literally prime the brain for abuse of other drugs.[22]

According to the recent studies mentioned above, the marijuana high is basically no different from a cocaine high. Dopamine levels rise sharply in response to marijuana, and the brain's ability to make dopamine can diminish over time, creating an even greater need for the drug. Since marijuana lingers in the blood for a long time, abrupt withdrawal of the kind seen in fast-acting drugs like nicotine does not occur. But recent studies suggest that many people who become addicted to marijuana continue to smoke not so much for the high as to relieve feelings of anxiety brought on by the drug itself.[23]

## MARIJUANA LAWS

Laws about marijuana have been the subject of controversy for many years. When marijuana use spread to the middle class in the 1960s and 1970s, public attitudes toward it softened. In 1970, President Richard Nixon created the National Commission on Marijuana and Drug Abuse. In 1972, the Commission issued its report, "Marijuana: A Signal of Misunderstanding." This report recommended the elimination of criminal penalties for possession of small amounts of marijuana.[24]

In 1977, President Jimmy Carter recommended federal marijuana decriminalization because of the harm being done to young people arrested for its use. However, even the National Organization for the Reform of Marijuana Laws (NORML), endorses the statement that adolescent marijuana use should be a legitimate concern for all Americans.[25]

Although some states adopted decriminalization laws, by the 1980s there was fear that marijuana was undermining the ability of children to compete effectively. There was a hardening of attitudes toward drug use by the end of the 1980s, when a survey showed that three quarters of all high school seniors disapproved of smoking marijuana. Ten years earlier, the percentage was only half.[26]

Some states that decriminalized small amounts of the drug for personal use recriminalized it by the 1990s. As a result, the number of people in prison for marijuana possession increased greatly.[27]

Millions of arrests have been made for marijuana law violations. It has been estimated that if marijuana were decriminalized or legalized, yearly arrests would be reduced by 500,000.[28] For some users and pushers, there is "revolving door" justice in which they are in and out of the criminal justice system quickly. For others, marijuana possession means real time in prison.

The legal history of marijuana laws is unusual. The Marijuana Tax Act of 1937 established the federal prohibition of marijuana. The drug was placed in Schedule I, which defines a substance as having a high potential for abuse, a lack of accepted safety for use under supervision, and no currently accepted medical use in treatment in the United States. Doctors are banned from writing prescriptions for marijuana. Opiate-based medications, which are stronger than marijuana, are in Schedule II and were never banned.[29]

Attempts have been made to move marijuana into Schedule II where doctors could prescribe it, but they were largely unsuccessful.

## MEDICINAL MARIJUANA

While those in favor of medicinal marijuana provide large amounts of data indicating the benefits of making it a prescription drug, government authorities and others counter with claims that the data is unscientific. Recently, the Office of National Drug Policy has pledged to consider more serious clinical research on medicinal marijuana.

Today, the medicinal value of marijuana is a subject of much controversy. According to many doctors, marijuana is a safe drug valuable for treatment in a number of diseases: in glaucoma, an eye disease common among the elderly; in cancer, to relieve the nausea that accompanies chemotherapy; in AIDS, to increase appetite of people whose bodies are wasting away; and in treating chronic pain, epilepsy, migraines, and other conditions.[30]

The most active ingredient in marijuana, THC, is available for medical use in pill form, but many patients claim that the drug is more effective when smoked. Between 1978 and 1996, 34 states plus the District of Columbia passed legislation recognizing marijuana's medicinal value. In 1996, California and Arizona voted to allow doctors to prescribe marijuana for patient use. Enforcement guidelines were issued to keep the new laws from fostering illegal use of the drug. Supporters of medical use of marijuana note that doctors' prescriptions for morphine appear to have little effect on the illegal use of morphine. Others note that heroin takes morphine's place in the drug culture, so this is not a valid argument.

In some areas there are medical Marijuana Buyers' Clubs, where people who are seriously ill join together to buy the drug even though they know they are breaking the law.

Whether or not the battle of medicinal marijuana is political or medical, one that will lead to problems or solve them, remains to be seen. Many drug prevention officials fear that allowing doctors to prescribe marijuana for medical use would sabotage the nation's "war on drugs." Would this lead to legalization or decriminalization and increase marijuana's use generally? Would it give the public a message that marijuana is safe?

Late in 1997, a group of experts who reviewed all the research available to date reported to the National Institutes of Health about marijuana's therapeutic value. In their forty-five-page report, they indicated that marijuana may counteract weight loss in people with AIDS, spasticity in those with multiple sclerosis and spinal cord injuries, and nausea among patients who are undergoing chemotherapy. They recommended controlled studies to find out if marijuana is useful, for whom, and how to use it.[31]

## MARIJUANA AND TEENS

While many things about marijuana remain controversial, even the most liberal supporters consider its use by adolescents harmful. It is possible that the increased popularity of marijuana is cyclical, and that this drug will become less popular as new information about its effects on the body is discovered. More is known about marijuana today than was known when many parents smoked it as teens. Some of the most important effects are noted by Joseph Califano, president of the National Center of Addiction and Substance Abuse at Columbia University: Marijuana can savage short-term memory and adversely affect motor skills. It inhibits social and emotional development at the time when such skills and development are most critical for teens. There are very real dangers attached to marijuana's frequent use.

# The Most Common Mind Drugs: Alcohol, Nicotine, and Caffeine

*Margaret O. Hyde*

**A**lcohol, nicotine, and caffeine are the drugs of choice among teens. While the first two are illegal drugs for minors, they are far more socially acceptable than marijuana, LSD, heroin, speed, and drugs that are illegal for adults, too. Caffeine is so well accepted that many people are surprised to learn that it is a drug.

## ALCOHOL

Middle school and high school students consume about 1.1 billion cans of beer each year.[1] In one recent month, half of the 2.8 million high school students had had a drink, and in one two-week period, about 30 percent of high school seniors were binge drinkers, having five or more drinks at one sitting.[2] Experts who are concerned about alcohol abuse say it is the number-one drug problem.

Many kids grow up knowing the different types of alcoholic beverages. When grain ferments, beer is produced.
When fruits ferment, wine is produced. Spirits (liquor) can
be distilled from fermented barley and other grains, pota-
toes, and sugar cane and molasses. Liquor has a higher alcohol content than wine or beer, but it is usually drunk in
smaller quantities. One 12-ounce lager beer, one 1° -ounce
shot of liquor, and one 5-ounce glass of wine have the same
amount of alcohol. "Aunt Millie can't be an alcoholic, she
only drinks wine," is a false statement.

Many alcoholic beverages have special appeal for the
young. Freeze and Squeeze, a frozen fruit juice that was
found at some grocery stores before officials had it removed,
contained 6 percent alcohol. Tumblers, a 24-proof blend of
fruit flavors and vodka, is popular with young people. Blend-
ers—ice cream cups with flavors like Pink Squirrel, Grass-
hopper, and Golden Cadillac—were introduced by The Ice
Cream Bar, a company based in Minneapolis. Each cup contains between 2 and 5 percent alcohol.[3]

*Drinking and Driving* Many beer drinkers say, "It's only
beer," without realizing how a six-pack can change their
ability to drive. Alcohol-related car crashes are the number-
one killer of teenagers in the United States. For young people,

inexperience in drinking and inexperience in driving make a deadly combination. Each day in 1996, eight young people died in alcohol-related crashes.[4]

Overall, drunk-driving deaths are rising again, according to Mothers Against Drunk Driving (MADD), and attention to the problem is waning. This group calls alcohol-related accidents "the nation's most frequently committed violent crime."[5]

How much alcohol makes a driver unsafe? Defining the amount of alcohol that will produce intoxication or decrease driving ability is difficult. The physical effects depend on the amount and frequency of the dosage plus mental and emotional effects that vary with the setting in which the drug is used and with the mood of the user. There is pressure to lower allowable limits in some states; experts feel this would save many lives.

Even a small amount of alcohol can create sensory impairment capable of causing injury or even death during activities such as driving, in-line skating, skateboarding, boating, and biking. Reports indicate that alcohol was associated with half of all unintentional injury victims, almost one quarter of suicide victims, and nearly half of all homicide deaths.[6]

***The Biology of Alcohol*** Although alcohol may cause relaxation at first, other effects—such as clumsiness, slurring of speech, and aggressive behavior—may follow continued drinking. The loss of inhibitions may lead to unprotected sex, which could in turn lead to AIDS, and/or unwanted pregnancy.

Sometimes people take a dare to consume large amounts of alcohol and die from alcohol poisoning (overdose). Although they are likely to become unconscious before this happens, the depression of various body systems can lead to coma and death. Death may also occur from suffocation related to vomiting brought on by drinking.[7]

# ABOUT ALCOHOL

*Alcohol abuse* is a pattern of problem drinking that results in health consequences, social problems, or both.

However, *alcohol dependence,* or *alcoholism,* refers to a disease that is characterized by abnormal alcohol-seeking behavior that leads to impaired control over drinking.

Short-term effects of alcohol use include:
- distorted vision, hearing, and coordination
- altered perceptions and emotions
- impaired judgment
- bad breath
- hangovers

Long-term effects of heavy alcohol use include:
- loss of appetite
- vitamin deficiencies
- stomach ailments
- skin problems
- sexual impotence
- liver damage
- heart and central nervous system damage
- memory loss

How do you know if you, or someone close, has a drinking problem?

Here are some quick clues:
- inability to control drinking— it seems that regardless of what you decide beforehand, you frequently wind up drunk
- using alcohol to escape problems
- a change in personality— turning from Dr. Jekyll to Mr. Hyde
- a high tolerance level—drinking just about everybody under the table
- blackouts—sometimes not remembering what happened while drinking
- problems at work or in school as a result of drinking
- concern shown by family and friends about drinking

If you have a drinking problem, or if you suspect you have a drinking problem, there are many others out there like you, and there is help available. Talk to a school counselor, a friend, or a parent.

Moderate amounts of alcohol, such as one drink for a woman and two for a man, may have some good effects. Alcohol causes a small reduction in fat levels, a small increase in good cholesterol, and it dilates the blood vessels. This can help prevent heart disease. However, the amount of alcohol consumed must be low enough so it does not cause liver damage or trigger heavier drinking.[8]

Every system in the body is affected by drinking. Although light drinking can lower the risk of heart disease, chronic heavy drinking is related to a variety of problems. The liver is especially vulnerable. Cirrhosis (a liver disease that can be brought on by too much alcohol), cancer, heart disease, and organic brain disease are some of the diseases that can result from heavy drinking.[9]

**Alcohol Addiction** The fact that alcohol is legal for adults helps to make drunkenness at any age better tolerated by society than other drug abuse. The earlier a person begins drinking, and the more a person drinks, the more likely he or she is to become an alcoholic.

---

**DRUG SCENE: ALCOHOL**
A waitress at the retirement community brings wine with dinner for all six of the elderly residents at the table, as she does every night. Their in-house physician recommended wine with dinner because she believes there is some therapeutic value in a small amount of daily alcohol. No one at the table considers this a drug scene, but it really is.

---

Alcoholism is an addiction and a disease that affects about 10 to 12 percent of the drinkers in the United States. Children of alcoholic parents have a greater chance of becoming addicted than others, because they may carry a genetic predisposition for the disease.

Other factors can lead to alcoholism, too. Family, school, workplace, and community conditions may play a part. The drug itself may be a major factor, since it can alter the body's neurochemistry and instill craving. Some people progress very quickly from social drinking to alcoholism, while others develop the disease over a period of decades.[10]

**Binge Drinking** Alcoholism may not depend on the amount of alcohol consumed, but on the way an individual drinks and the effect alcohol has on the person.[11] Many young people drink to get drunk. They may drink heavily only on the weekends and think there is no problem, even though falling grades and antisocial behavior are common for binge drinkers.

Some college fraternities around the nation have made changes in the way alcohol is treated at parties. Some are even going dry.[12] A number of colleges have turned to peer pressure to curb drinking and find that binge drinking drops when students learn that not everybody does it. But binge drinking is still popular in spite of the fact that about twenty-five fraternity youths have drunk themselves to death in the past dozen years.[13] Most students learn to moderate their drinking behavior before college graduation, but some become alcoholics.[14]

Because alcoholism is largely a hidden disease, no one knows how many deaths result from it. Some experts estimate 100,000 deaths each year, but others believe the number is much larger. Certainly, alcohol is a strong psychoactive drug that can be enjoyed by adults when used in small amounts. But even low alcohol use is probably not safe for people who are under legal drinking age, are pregnant, have a high genetic or environmental susceptibility to addiction, or are allergic to it.[15]

# NICOTINE

"Tobacco use is the greatest risk factor affecting the global disease burden in the world," according to the World Health Organization and the Harvard School of Medicine.[16]

The first reports on the dangers of smoking were published in 1859, but 1997 was the year in which the nation finally took large-scale action to prevent the harm caused by nicotine.

Joe Camel, the popular cartoon figure created by R.J. Reynolds Tobacco Company, "died" after years of promoting cigarettes in ads that were credited with attracting children to smoke Camels. In 1986, this brand's market share in underage smokers was less than 3 percent. In 1988, Joe Camel was introduced, and by 1993, Camel's youth market share had grown to 13 percent.[17] According to some anti-tobacco activists, Joe Camel was almost as well known to children as Walt Disney's Mickey Mouse.

---

### DRUG SCENE: NICOTINE

Eight-year-olds Brian and Carlos smoke the cigarettes they stole from the local drug store on their way to school. They manage to get to school on time, and during the day they work on their English report about the hazards of smoking. They think it may be true that some people get addicted to tobacco, but they are certain it won't happen to them.

---

Young adults now see ads with Marlboro Man lookalikes in which the text says he has emphysema (a lung disease). Kids are bombarded with information about the dangers of smoking, but the percentage of eighth, tenth, and twelfth graders who smoke daily is rising.[18] While 50 percent of high school seniors may smoke, 50 percent do not. So not everyone smokes.

# About Cigarette Smoking

Although many people smoke because they believe cigarettes calm their nerves, smoking releases epinephrine, a hormone that actually creates psychological stress in the smoker, rather than relaxation.

The use of tobacco is addictive. Most users develop tolerance for nicotine and need greater amounts to produce a desired effect. Smokers become physically and psychologically dependent and will suffer withdrawal symptoms including: changes in body temperature, heart rate, digestion, muscle tone, and appetite.

Psychological symptoms may include:
• irritability and anxiety
• sleep disturbances
• nervousness
• headaches
• fatigue
• nausea
• cravings for tobacco that can last days, weeks, months, years, or even an entire lifetime.

Risks associated with smoking cigarettes:
• diminished or extinguished sense of smell and taste
• frequent colds
• smoker's cough
• gastric ulcers
• chronic bronchitis
• increase in heart rate and blood pressure
• premature and more abundant face wrinkles
• emphysema
• heart disease
• stroke
• cancer of the mouth, larynx, pharynx, esophagus, lungs, pancreas, cervix, uterus, and bladder

Cigarette smoking is perhaps the most devastating preventable cause of disease and premature death.

Smoking is particularly dangerous for teens because their bodies are still developing and changing and the 4,000 chemicals (including 200 known poisons) in cigarette smoke can adversely affect this process.

While some students will respond to "Mind if I smoke?" with "Care if I die?," many feel that they are invincible. Marta visited her grandmother in a nursing home after her grandmother's cancer operation. Marta's grandmother had been trying to stop smoking for many years, but even cancer did not stop her. She managed to smoke through the hole in her throat after she lost one lung and part of her mouth. Marta said she would not let that happen to her. She would smoke until she was in her thirties, then she would stop. She believed her body could deal with any problems because she was young.

As smoking comes under attack by adults, it becomes more attractive to some kids who think it is a good way to rebel against their parents. Being cool is more important to them than future health. Hollywood and the music world have played a large part in glamorizing cigarettes. They never mention the victims who end up in cancer wards. But today many young people agree that it is cool to *not* smoke.

**Cigars and Smokeless Tobacco** Cigars have become part of the fabric of hip city life in spite of the fact that many consider their taste and odor unpleasant. They are cited as making a person feel sexy and sensual, in power and in control. The American Cancer Society has produced a public service ad suggesting that fancy cigar cutters might come in handy for excising lip tumors. The cigar trend may be short-lived as prices rise, quality goes down, and the antismoking messages hit home.

Smokeless tobacco is popular with many boys and girls. Two kinds, moist snuff and dry leaf, supply nicotine, can become addictive, and can cause cancer of the mouth. Some baseball players who were noted for their habit of chewing smokeless tobacco have substituted gum, partly to protect themselves and partly so they will not set a bad example for the kids who admire them. For those who know what smokeless tobacco can do to the human body, chewing is no longer "in."

Health activists hope the whole smoking trend will eventually run out of cool as more and more young people get the antismoking message.


## CAFFEINE

The majority of people who drink coffee, tea, and cola drinks enjoy them in moderation without serious adverse effects. Many doctors tell their patients to drink decaffeinated coffee for health reasons, especially if they have problems with their hearts or digestive systems.

Tolerance to caffeine does occur, but it varies with different people. About six cups of coffee a day, ten cola drinks, or eight cups of tea can result in dependence or addiction. Withdrawal symptoms can occur after long-term use of just a few cups a day.[19] These symptoms can include headache, sleepiness, and lethargy.

Deaths and near-deaths due to caffeine poisoning have happened, but they are very infrequent. Drinking too much coffee is not a cause of these deaths, since it is virtually impossible to ingest life-threatening amounts of caffeine in beverage form. Caffeine tablets and medicine containing caffeine are responsible for the lethal doses.[20]

*Caffeine in Popular Drinks* Caffeine experts cite the widespread use of coffee, cola drinks, water, and other drinks spiked with caffeine as making it the most widely used mind drug. After a period in which clear and no-caffeine drinks were popular, the trend toward caffeinated soft drinks and coffee is back. Many teens socialize at coffee shops instead of the soda fountains that attracted their parents.

Mountain Dew is one of the best-selling drinks in the United States, partly due to its caffeine content.[21] Surge has more caffeine than Classic Coca-Cola. Josta has a bit more caffeine than Surge or Mountain Dew. Teenagers are the target of many beverage makers who produce drinks that carry an extra caffeine kick.

***Chocolate*** Caffeine from chocolate is a popular mood-altering food, and craving for chocolate is common. Some people have difficulty getting through a whole day without eating chocolate in some form or other. People who binge on chocolate do not realize that they have a drug habit.

For most young people, indulgence in caffeine as a mind drug is pleasant, but overindulgence can exacerbate insomnia, cardiovascular and gastrointestinal problems, and anxiety. Caffeine is so irritating to the stomach that many people who drink coffee have indigestion most of the time.[22]

Nicotine use by adults is declining as society changes its view of smoking from being "cool" to causing a public health problem. Attitudes about alcohol abuse are changing, too. According to some predictions, caffeine will be the drug of choice for the new-millennium generation.

# The Legalization
# Controversy
*Margaret O. Hyde*

**D**o you think the government has a right to control your personal drug use? Narcotics officers and drug users usually have very different ideas about this, but you and the rest of the general public will cast the vote that makes mind drugs legal or keeps them illegal.

Opinions range from trying to make America drug free to making all drugs legal. Do you think cocaine should be sold in a state-controlled liquor store if there were rules to prohibit sales to children? What about marijuana? Should it be sold with the same restrictions that apply to cigarettes? Would this mean an increase in the amount of drug use?

No one has all the answers to the many questions about the legalization of drugs, but there are many opinions and some conflicting evidence. Some highly respected, conservative individuals have joined liberals who call for a change in drug policy, and proposals for legalizing drugs have entered the mainstream of public debate.[1]

## LEGALIZATION, DECRIMINALIZATION, OR REGULATION?

Many people who argue vehemently about the merits or the tragedy of legalizing drugs are not really clear about what they favor.[2] Legalization means different things to different people, and even though the general climate appears to be against the legalization of drugs, there is a definite trend to either legalize or decriminalize drugs.[3]

Of the 300 organizations throughout the world that support drug law reform, some groups stand for legalizing all drugs while others want decriminalization of certain drugs, usually marijuana. Decriminalization means that someone arrested for possession of a small amount of a drug such as marijuana would be tried in a civil court rather than a criminal court.

Rather than legalization or decriminalization, according to some activists, government regulation is the way to go. In this approach, certain drugs are made available to addicts in government-run clinics.[4] For example, in Switzerland, there is state distribution of heroin to hardened addicts. In September 1997, Swiss voters overwhelmingly endorsed their government's liberal drug policies.[5]

Legalizing some drugs with certain restrictions, similar to those on tobacco and alcohol, has considerable appeal to many users and lawmakers. But some ask if tobacco and alcohol would be legalized in today's climate, when the effects of these drugs on the human body are better understood. Would legalizing only some illicit drugs be a logistical nightmare?

You will probably be asked to cast your vote on the question of legalization in the near future. Even though you may be tired of hearing messages about the drug war, you may need to sort out what you think you know from what you really do know.


## CHANGING LAWS

Laws about mind-altering drugs have come and gone through the years. Nettie, a grandmother who advocates the legalization of marijuana for medical reasons, remembers when this drug was legal and alcohol was not. Fifteen-year-old Tom is surprised to learn that his mother bought amphetamines at the drugstore as diet pills when she was a teen. Tom buys these drugs on the black market.

At one time, all mind drugs were legal. Some became illegal for a number of different reasons, including morality, public safety, concern for the health of users and nonusers, and even as a reaction against foreigners. Talk of a "yellow peril" and "oriental depravity" played a part in outlawing the opium dens described in chapter 2.

Some of the old laws, such as those that closed opium dens, were enacted before much was known about how drugs affect the human body. The Harrison Narcotic Act was adopted in 1914 amid fears of violence from drug-addicted minorities and criminals. It was meant to regulate the sale of opium and cocaine, but the legislation ultimately banned most mind drugs for all but medical use.

Although alcohol was not generally considered a drug, an amendment to the Constitution outlawed its use in 1920. In a climate of bootleggers and speakeasies, Prohibition was repealed in 1933 as unenforceable. Advocates of laws against drug use say that there was less drinking during that period. Others blame Prohibition for disrespect of the law as well as huge growth in criminal activity.

*Can Drug Abuse Be Controlled by Laws?* Many drug laws were enacted by 1970, but drug abuse continued to grow. In one of many efforts to overcome the nation's drug problem, the government created an agency called the Office of National Drug Control Policy. This provided a strategy for implementing many drug laws. The Omnibus Anti-Drug Act of 1986 classified drugs into schedules according to how a drug is used medically, how safe it is, and its potential for abuse. As knowledge grew, some drugs were rescheduled.

Attempts to prevent drug abuse by enacting more laws have been compared to the story of Sisyphus, a Greek god whose task was to roll a huge rock up a mountain. Every time he nearly reached the summit, the rock rolled down the mountain. But he tried again and again, hoping he would succeed. Many people feel that trying to prevent drug abuse with laws is just as hopeless, but others feel that good progress has been made.[6]

According to an annual survey released by the government in 1997, illicit drug use is still unacceptably high, but there is a glimmer of hope.[7] According to another survey released the same year, drug use among teenagers was found to have increased.[8] Different surveys produce different results, partly because it is difficult to collect honest information about illegal activities. One survey of drug use by young people is called Monitoring the Future. It is conducted at the University of Michigan and has been carried out each year since 1975.

Some experts say the government should heed the old folk wisdom, "If you are in a hole, stop digging." They say new laws are only a way of digging deeper.

The question of whether or not to legalize drugs is complex, and the potential costs and benefits need considerable study. Many important details are not considered in the general arguments. For example, which drugs might be legalized? How would they be sold? Where would they be sold? What restrictions would apply? Would advertising be permitted? In what form would drugs be made available? The question of drug legalization does not lend itself to simplistic debate.

The same arguments about whether or not drugs should be legalized are used again and again. When you read the following pages, consider that the conditions for controlling access to the many different abused drugs could consume years of debate in legislatures.

***Would Legalization Save Money?*** Fighting drugs is big business. Federal, state, and local governments spend billions of dollars each year in efforts to patrol borders, arrest and punish users and dealers, research the effects of drugs and ways to educate the public about the hazards of drugs, treat addicts, and care for addicts and their children.[9]

Keeping one person in prison for one year costs taxpayers between $16,000 and $20,000, several times what it costs to educate one child. FBI figures show that nearly 600,000 Americans were arrested on marijuana charges in 1995.[10] The government spends about $7 billion a year enforcing marijuana laws.[11]

Arrests for drug crimes have greatly increased during the past two decades. The number of arrests for drug abuse violations increased by 120 percent from 1992 to 1996.[12] In 1996, 25 percent of prisoners were incarcerated for drug charges.[13] Certainly, the overcrowding of courts and prisons with drug offenders has contributed to a growing movement for the legalization of mind drugs.

According to its advocates, legalization makes economic sense in another way, too. Attempting to seal the borders is extremely expensive and there is controversy about whether or not the confiscation of huge amounts of drugs has much effect on the problem. Enough heroin to supply all the addicts in the United States can be made from opium poppies grown on only twenty square miles of land. A year's supply of cocaine can be stashed in thirteen truck trailers. So, no matter how much illegal drugs are seized as they come across the borders, the supply will always be enough to meet the demand.[14]

Money saved by legalization could be used to expand prevention and treatment programs for addicts. It could provide more help for agencies that attack poverty, racism, unemployment, and other problems that contribute to the spread of drug addiction.[15]

If government taxes on drug sales were substantial, pure drugs could still be provided at prices well below current levels.[16] Money from taxes on legalized drugs could be another plus for legalization.

However, according to basic economic principles, increasing availability and decreasing price will increase the demand for a commodity. Herbert D. Kleber, former deputy director of the Office of National Drug Control Policy, suggests that the legalization of cocaine might result in cocaine use being nine times higher.[17]

In addition to the increased cost for the nation if drug use increases, the human side must be considered. It is estimated that legalization would result in 100,000 to 500,000 drug-induced deaths each year. This is not counting nicotine, which is responsible for about 400,000 deaths each year.

Taxes on legalized drugs could create a black market supported by people who want to avoid paying the tax. Money would be needed for more police and courts to combat this black market. Taxes paid on drugs might not even be economically beneficial. The tax on alcohol today amounts to far less than the money spent caring for alcoholics.

How much drug abuse would increase is unknown. If there were a great increase as predicted by those who argue against legalization, huge amounts of money would be needed to treat addicts. If a dose of cocaine cost less than $.50 it would be well within the reach of ten-year-olds. The introduction of cheap cocaine in the form of crack illustrates this. When it became available in small doses for $3 to $5 a rock, the use of crack cocaine exploded. This argument indicates that the number of users would increase and the cost of treatment would be staggering.[18]

Legalizers have not proposed exactly how drugs would be produced, distributed, and licensed, or how a black market could be controlled. Legalization may be no less expensive than the current prohibition.[19]

**Would Legalization Remove the Criminal Element?** If drugs were legal, addicts would no longer have to commit crimes in order to obtain them. Through the years, the demand for illegal mind drugs has spawned and supported a huge criminal network of growing, manufacturing, importing, and distributing the drugs. The size of the illegal drug business has grown into billions of dollars. Since drugs are illegal, drug distributors and dealers cannot go to court to solve disputes. They solve many of them by shooting each other. Drive-by shootings often miss their targets, and in some neighborhoods many innocent people are killed. Addicts seeking money for drugs add to the crime problem by stealing, mugging, and sometimes killing. Many addicts who would have no connection with the criminal world are drawn into it to support their habits. In some cases, police and government officials are bribed by drug dealers who threaten to harm their families.

Many poor people become involved in selling drugs or in smuggling them into the country. Those who carry packets of drugs on and in their bodies are called mules, and they are subject to arrest if caught. (In some cases, mules who swallow condoms filled with drugs die when a condom bursts and highly potent drugs enter their bloodstreams.)

Criminals would no longer make such large sums of money if drugs were legal. Today, the profit on drugs can exceed 5,000 times a drug's original cost.[20]

Money laundering—hiding the source of cash by channeling it through various accounts to avoid exposure to law enforcement agents—is a major criminal enterprise. Because it is illegal, the drug business is a cash business. Drug barons are believed to launder as much a $100 billion a year from profits they make in the United States.[21] Legalization would do away with extensive money laundering and the money now pouring into illegitimate drugs would be directed toward legitimate businesses.

According to Barbara Ehrenreich, a well-known writer, the federal government has squandered billions of dollars trying to enforce drug laws. This prohibition, she says, has made the drug trade more lucrative, allowing the Mafia and street gangs to flourish. She believes that decriminalization or legalization would be less harmful.[22]

After legalization, drugs would still be illegal for children and young adults, and the young would be targets for black marketers. Advertisements probably would be subtly aimed to encourage children to try drugs. The problem of controlling alcohol and tobacco advertising that appears to be slanted toward the young is recognized today. Would there be subtle ways of encouraging children to try cocaine, marijuana, and other drugs on the legitimate market?

No matter how many different mind drugs were sold through legal channels, chemists could introduce new ways of getting high and sell these drugs on the black market. Many legal plants and chemicals that produce highs are available today, and some are far more potent that common illegal drugs. Many species of mushrooms that grow wild throughout most of the United States can be used as mind drugs, and they cannot be controlled.[23] New chemical combinations that are synthesized for drug use have already found their way into the black market.

If drug abuse increases after legalization, there may be far more crime, not less.[24] Traffickers are well organized and well financed. They adjust to any action taken against them and can find many ways of making money from people who wish to experiment with drugs or who are addicted.

***Would Legalization Improve Public Health?*** Many drug users die from toxic substances that are used to dilute illegal narcotics and from overdoses when drugs are more potent than represented. Government control on the production of these drugs could make certain they were pure and standardize them so that their strength would not be in question.

Addicts could have more access to medical care in a society that accepted them and could have a better chance for treatment programs. Addiction would be recognized as a disease rather than as a crime, so the stigma would be lessened and closet addicts would be more likely to seek help.

But an increase in drug use through legalization could mean a large public health problem. With drugs more easily available, no one knows how many more young people who experiment would make drug abuse a way of life.

The health of nonusers would be affected, too. Doctors are already concerned about the effect of secondhand tobacco smoke on children, but they are even more concerned about the effect of crack and other drugs. The passive inhalation of crack smoke can cause seizures and other neurological symptoms in infants and toddlers.

Another problem is that legalizing drugs may foster their use. Many young people say they do not use illegal drugs for fear of being imprisoned, but they use tobacco and alcohol even though they are illegal for their age group.

**Would Legalization Protect Individual Rights?** Legalizers say, "It's my body and I have a right to do what I please so long as I am the only one affected."

Few people still use this argument because it is obvious that drug abuse does affect others in many ways. However, many people who are forced to take drug tests in order to participate in sports or to keep a job resent the invasion of their privacy. Some tests are inaccurate. People can test positive as the result of certain legal drugs or because of mistakes in records.

In 1994, the United States Supreme Court ruled that drug testing of athletes was constitutional and does not violate a person's rights. Drugs in the workplace are believed to have a serious effect on safety, performance, and morale. Those who defend drug testing in the workplace believe that occasional testing will prevent many workers from taking drugs that may result in harm to themselves and others.

Drug use dropped dramatically in the military after random drug testing began. Today, a recruit must test negative for drugs before entering the armed forces. Pilots and train engineers began to be tested for drugs following accidents that appeared to be drug related. Even many of those who support legalization of drugs do not object to this kind of testing.

Two of the drugs that cause major problems for users and those around them are legal. Drunk driving and alcoholism are responsible for numerous deaths. Nicotine is responsible for more deaths than illegal drugs.

We have looked at just some of the arguments for and against legalization. No one really knows whether or not legalization would lower the demand for drugs, save money, or improve public health. It would be a big step and there are no easy solutions.

# Now The Good Part Begins: Alternatives to Drug Abuse

## Allan Y. Cohen, Ph.D.

Dr. Cohen is Executive Director, Pacific Institute for Research and Evaluation, and Associate Editor of the Journal of Primary Prevention. He is a former drug user who stopped all illegal use of drugs after becoming disillusioned with their promise.

"**W**hy would you want to use drugs?" asked the psychologist. His client looked him straight in the eye and asked back, "Why not?"

A lot of time and money have been spent trying to find out why people use drugs. Reading some of the articles in this book, you begin to get the idea that there are all kinds of causes for drug abuse—social and economic problems, personality difficulties, family hassles, boredom, curiosity, escape, excitement, pressure from peers, and many, many more. We realize that people have been raised in different environments. They have different needs and different motives, and they may grow up with different attitudes about taking chemical substances—whether cigarettes, alcohol, prescription medicine, or illegal drugs.

## BACKGROUNDS

Americans use an incredible amount of legal and illegal drugs. Adults seem to prefer abusing the legal variety—alcohol, tranquilizers, nicotine in tobacco, or stimulants like diet pills. Somehow people seem to have lost respect for the natural efficiency of their own bodies and minds. When they feel sick or mentally worried, the first thing they think of is "medicine."

Billions of doses of dangerous mind drugs are prescribed by doctors, sometimes because the doctors don't know how to handle normal psychological problems, sometimes because the patients demand some kind of medication. Most researchers estimate that more than half the American adult population has a serious problem with the abuse of mind drugs.

Social scientists have almost given up some of their pet theories about the "weird" drug user. It now seems clear that we are a drug-using society, a civilization that considers drug use natural and looks to external aids for the solution of internal problems. The use of mind drugs is a *style*, a style reinforced by adult behavior, by pharmaceutical company media advertising, and by the idea that all medical problems should be cured by drugs.

Drug users range from those who are just curious experimenters to those who are completely hooked. Most of the publicity in the early 1970s centered on heroin addiction, on the narcotic-dependent "junkie" often involved in crime to support the demanding habit. But heroin use is merely the tip of an iceberg. Other mind drugs might not be as dramatically addicting, but their effects can be dangerous, partly because they can also be subtle. New findings on the effects of THC, the principal active chemical in "grass" and "hash," suggest that it may have accumulative negative effects on the nervous system and especially on the personality and mind.

Heavy users, who smoke more than once a week, may have some cumulative effects. Since these effects occur gradually, they never suspect that the cause is marijuana or hashish. In fact, some of the so-called "softer drugs" have a remarkable ability to interfere with the mind's natural "feedback" ability. Judgment is impaired because substances like marijuana can easily allow a person to fool themselves about how well they are doing.

## ALTERNATIVES TO DRUGS

People continue to take drugs even when they are aware of unhealthful side effects. The classic case is cigarette smoking—the "mature" adults in our society have shown a remarkable resistance to giving up cigarettes, even though they know the health hazards involved.

This type of behavior helps us to understand a "mystery" about drug abuse that may point the way to some solutions. The secret is an observation often overlooked because it is so simple: *people use drugs because they want to.* They get some enjoyment from drugs, even if the enjoyment is temporary. People use drugs in the hope of feeling better, whatever that might mean for each individual. Unfortunately, most drugs seem to exact a more precious price than the "high" they give, the fun they provide, or the relief they temporarily produce.

Psychologists and educators say to drug users, "You know that drugs are bad for you, physically and mentally! You've seen the damage that drugs have done to friends of yours! But you keep doing it. How can we convince you to stop?" The young person takes it all in and quietly challenges, "Show me something better!"

This tells us a lot about preventing drug abuse before it destroys a person's chance to make a life for themselves. People *will stop* using drugs as soon as they find *something better*. People are not as likely to *start* serious drug abuse if they have *something better going for them*. The "something better" is what we might call an *alternative to drugs*. The common denominator of all successful drug abuse prevention and treatment programs is their ability to provide the potential user, the experimenter, or the addict with meaningful and satisfying alternatives.

## REASONS FOR NOT USING DRUGS

| BIGGEST DETERRENT FOR NOT USING DRUGS | PERCENTAGE OF STUDENTS* |
|---|---|
| 1. No need (i.e., life is fine, I'm happy, or I turn on other ways) | 39.8 |
| 2. Concern about interfering with physical and mental health and athletics | 22.4 |
| 3. Because of the laws (i.e., respect for the law or fear of getting busted) | 7.1 |
| 4. Brains and good judgment (i.e., having them) | 6.2 |
| 5. Fear of the unknown | 6.0 |
| 6. Seen results in other people | 4.9 |
| 7. Out of love and respect for parents | 4.4 |
| 8. Fear of addiction | 3.4 |
| 9. Friends (i.e., peer pressure against drug use) | 3.2 |
| 10. Other (not yet been contacted to take drugs, personal values or religion, unfavorable past experience, poor quality of drugs, don't know, etc.) | 10.2 |

* Percentage adds up to over 100 percent because of some multiple answers.

When we talk about "alternatives" to drugs, we do not mean the same thing as "substitutes" for drugs. One crutch is not necessarily better than another. A young heroin addict might give up "junk" in order to join a violent street gang; this might be a substitute, but it is not a very constructive alternative. Another thing to realize about alternatives is that no one alternative is relevant for everyone. There is a pertinent saying in the drug field: "Different strokes for different folks." We know that people abuse drugs for different motives and needs. Sometimes these motives and needs come from *deficiency,* from serious problems. But other times there are *positive* needs causing drug experimentation, like the desire for adventure, curiosity, or the urge to explore oneself. Since people have varying needs and aspirations, the alternatives replacing drugs must also vary.

Generally, alternatives must be stronger as drug dependency gets stronger. The hard-core heroin addict has to be faced with a very involving alternative. Many successful former addicts have undergone deep spiritual conversions. Others have been rehabilitated through a tightly controlled residential therapeutic community where they could neither obtain drugs nor kid anybody about who they were.

When children first start out in school, it is possible to provide them with much subtler alternatives like a real joy for learning, respect for themselves and their bodies, and the ability to understand and enjoy other children. The more people have good feelings about themselves, the better they can appreciate and relate to others; the more they know what is important in their lives, the less attraction the drug experience will have for them. It is not so much that drug-free people are afraid of drugs—educators have not been successful in *scaring* students out of drug use—it is more that they have better things to do than getting "stoned" with chemicals.

When some teachers and students decided to get together to do a drug survey at a high school near San Francisco, a questionnaire was devised and circulated by students; replies were anonymous. At that time, about half the students were using drugs. In addition to other questions, the *nonusers* (about 400) were asked the question, "If you do *not* use drugs, what has been the biggest deterrent for not using them?" The 260 completed responses to this open-ended question were categorized and gave the results shown in Table I (page 000).

This table shows a very interesting trend—the greatest percentage of reasons given reflect *positive* reasons for not using drugs; only a few mentioned fear of something bad happening. It turns out that natural alternatives compete very well against drugs. If they are given a chance these alternatives are usually found to be preferable to the temporary and artificial chemical experience.

## TYPES OF ALTERNATIVES TO DRUGS

There is one primary step in promoting this new approach to the drug problem—getting people to think about alternatives and to apply the principle to themselves. A parallel trend we see is a new appreciation of the natural environment. The beauty and desirability of unspoiled air, water, and open space is increasingly a matter of concern. Ever since the 1960s, Americans have become more and more alert to the necessity for avoiding and reducing pollution. The same consciousness has been turning to the purity of foods and the undesirability of artificial and perhaps dangerous ingredients. Today, more and more people are becoming aware of "health pollution" and are trying to be moderate in drug use as well as avoiding other toxic chemicals.

Before mentioning other types of alternatives, it might be good to mention one alternative rarely discussed—the discontinuance of drug use. Many moderate drug users find that they feel much better (physically and mentally) after they stop their drug use. Even long-term users of marijuana report rather dramatic improvements (according to their own judgments) three to twelve weeks after they stop using mind drugs.

Of course, the structure of our social institutions has much to do with whether or not many kinds of alternatives are available to the general public. Part of the more general cause of the drug-use explosion has been the inability of government and society to meet adequately individuals' legitimate aspirations. These same deficiencies in society make the application of viable alternatives very difficult and slow. A good example of this is our elementary and secondary school systems. With some real exceptions, school is likely to be an uninspiring and sometimes meaningless experience for many students. In many places, the school curriculum is built around the world of students of twenty years ago. Many schools still stress competition and the importance of grades; this interferes with the joy of learning. Much of the material covered in the classroom has little application to the practical problems encountered by students. Many teachers are very reluctant to explore the area of students' *feelings*, yet the emotional and mental state of students is critically important when decisions about drug use have to be made.

In a true "alternative school" situation, teachers are allowed to innovate and get "turned on" by the subject, thereby transferring this enthusiasm to students. Since teachers are possible models, they would, ideally, be relatively free from drug dependency and be able to communicate the feeling of the "natural high." Students would be given feedback, but not graded—especially in so-called extracurricular areas like art, music, physical education, manual arts, computer science, homemaking, drama, etc. After all, students should be able to develop real interests in leisure or career activities, freed from the debilitating pressure and anxiety that comes from worrying about how good one is at a particular subject. If a person finds something valuable in his or her life—whether it is a hobby, a talent, a purpose, other people—the lure of drugs loses its luster.

## EXAMPLES OF NATURAL ALTERNATIVES

In order to be more specific, let us look at examples of natural alternatives. One way of categorizing alternatives involves *areas of experience*. These areas of experience—from physical to spiritual—correspond to the kinds of gratification people seek when they use drugs. There is a lack in some area of experience and people try to use drugs to fill that deficiency.

One level is the *physical*. A person may use drugs to try to improve his or her sense of physical well-being. Examples of alternatives might include the following: dance and movement training; physical recreation, including athletics, exercise, hiking, and nature exploration; relaxation exercises, physical *(hatha)* yoga; and proper training in the martial arts, such as aikido, karate, judo.

Some people use drugs to gain satisfaction in the *sensory* area—involving the desire to enhance or stimulate sight, hearing, touch, or taste. Examples of alternatives include such things as: training in sensory awareness (balance, co-ordination, small-muscle control, and so on); visual exploration of nature; and the learning and practice of responsible sexuality.

One of the areas most commonly stressed in the study of drug abuse is the *emotional* level of experience. Some people might turn to drugs to gain relief from psychological pain, in an attempt to solve personal problems, or to eliminate anxiety or gain some measure of emotional relaxation. Natural alternatives in this area might include: getting a trusted professional to give counseling or psychotherapy; educational instruction in the psychology of personal development; and emotional awareness exercises, such as learning "body language," self-awareness, and psychological awareness.

A key area of alternatives is the *interpersonal*. It is no secret that many use drugs to try to gain acceptance and status from friends and peers or to break through interpersonal barriers of one kind or another. Natural alternatives include a whole host of possibilities, some being: getting into a group of friends who are not serious drug users; experiencing well-run group therapy or counseling sessions; family life education and training; emotional tutoring—for example, big brothers and sisters helping younger people; and creation of community "rap centers."

A rarer type of gratification sought by drug users involves the *mental* or *intellectual* level. They try to escape mental boredom, gain new understanding in the world of ideas, study better, or satisfy intellectual curiosity. Drug-induced insight is rarely enlightening—the author knows of a respected scientist who made an incredible "discovery" under LSD; for weeks afterward he walked the streets telling everyone he saw that "two plus two equals four!" Examples of more natural possibilities are intellectual excitement through reading, discussion, creative games and puzzles; training in hypnosis under qualified teachers; creativity training; and memory training.

Depending on the types of drugs that become popular from year to year, one might hear talk about the *creative* or *aesthetic* level of experience related to drugs. People tried to enhance their experience or productivity in the arts. (Some people still cannot stand to go to a concert unless they are high.) Yet natural alternatives work out better for the artist or appreciator of art and music. Alternatives might include: nongraded instruction in the performing or appreciation of music; creative hobbies, such as crafts, sewing, cooking, gardening, and photography; and experience in communications skills such as writing, public speaking, conversation.

Another subtle level might be called *stylistic*. Here the user is caught up in certain styles, or the need to identify through imitation of adults or the desire for achieving things instantly. Alternatives can include: exposure to others who are meaningfully involved in nonchemical alternatives; agreement by parents cut down on their own drug use; and exposure to the philosophy of the natural, appreciating the great possibilities of inner human resources.

An area often overlooked, but with great potential for dissatisfied drug experimenters, is the *social,* including the notion of *service to others.* Some may be desperate about our social and political situation and try to forget it or rebel against it through the fog of drugs. The alternatives are not only more constructive, but can be very fulfilling on a personal level. In the political area, people can be involved and work for particular candidates or in nonpartisan political projects, as in lobbying for environmental groups. One of the most powerful sets of alternatives, available to almost everyone, consists of getting involved in social service—helping others.[1] This could include: helping the poor; providing companionship to the lonely; helping those in trouble with drugs or family problems; or helping out in voluntary organizations (like YMCA and YWCA, Girl Scouts, Boys' Clubs, Big Brothers and Sisters, and so on).

Another experiential level, the *spiritual* or *mystical,* attracted many users of psychedelics. Psychologists and sociologists are beginning to discover that they underestimated the power of the drive for spirituality. Some people hoped that drugs would give them direct spiritual experience, going beyond the limits of orthodox religion; they hoped to get a vision of God. For these people drugs can be very seductive because certain chemicals can induce illusory religious experiences that seem very real to the user. A user may be temporarily inspired, but too often chases after this mirage and cannot apply what he or she thought were profound mystical insights. In contrast, growing in popularity are nonchemical methods for spiritual understanding and experience. These include such approaches as: study of spiritual literature; meditation and yoga; contemplation and prayer; spiritual song and dance; and increased exposure to different techniques of applied spirituality. In the spiritual area as well as the other areas, not every alternative offered is of the highest quality. As we become more sophisticated about alternative means of inner growth, we shall become better able to tell the really helpful approaches from the hollow or misleading ones.

The examples given above do not cover every level of experience; indeed, some readers might like to categorize alternatives in very different ways. There are some examples that we might call *miscellaneous*. These relate to other needs, such as the need for risk-taking and danger, the desire for adventure or exploration, the need for economic success, and combinations of various other motives. Here one might think of alternatives such as: sky diving, scuba diving, and "Outward Bound" survival training; vocational counseling that will lead to meaningful employment; and the possibility of gaining school credits for actual work experience in the community.

## HINTS FOR THE ALTERNATIVES SEEKER

The use of mind drugs demands that people be *passive* and *uninvolved*. The lure of chemical intervention is that you can get something for nothing—by swallowing, smoking, or injecting you get happiness at a low price. But the evidence shows the contrary. When you possesses the drug style, it possesses you back. But it is not always fair to criticize the drug user. After all, he or she is merely falling for the cultural line, going along with the prevailing philosophy that deep down, people are not really worth that much and have to be enhanced by some outside agent.

But times are changing. A few years ago, in many circles, it was more hip to use drugs, now it is beginning to be more hip to go beyond drugs. But how does one choose the way of going beyond? For some, it is no big problem—drugs are not that attractive; life is involving and meaningful, if not always easy. Other searchers may not be getting much help from their families, schools, or communities, who may not recognize the need to assist in providing alternatives.

The individual searcher must be alert. A person who wants to be happier and more fulfilled, must *try*. A great alternative in itself is the *process of putting energy into finding alternatives.* There are other guidelines that may be helpful. Be optimistic. If you have used drugs, ask yourself what you enjoyed about the drug experience; ask what areas in your life need work and fulfillment. Then *seek,* particularly in the areas of your highest interest. That means asking about different alternatives you hear about or read about. Follow up leads, investigate possibilities. One useful way is to discover the secrets of those you really admire—whether friends, peers, or heroes—in order to find out what turns *them* on. It can help to ask anyone who might know about interesting avenues of exploration, especially former drug users. Look for help and ask for help if you need it. Stay off drugs as much as possible while looking; it will help you evaluate the alternatives. Get others to join you in the search. Have faith in both yourself and in the possibilities of natural alternatives.

The problem of drug abuse is both a tragedy and a challenge. It raises issues that every responsible human being should face. The search for viable alternatives can be, at the same time, great fun and very profound. When honestly faced, the challenge of self-discovery can force new perspectives on the game of life. In the words of the great Indian spiritual leader Meher Baba, "To penetrate into the essence of all being and significance and to release the fragrance of that inner attainment for the guidance and benefit of others, by expressing, in the world of forms, truth, love, purity and beauty—this is the sole game which has intrinsic and absolute worth."[2]

# Afterword—Chill: The Decision Is Yours

*Margaret O. Hyde*

The controversy over the "war on drugs" and how to wage it has been going on for decades. Kids laugh at some of the messages that adults use to try to scare them from drug abuse. Many kids know that reefer madness is a joke. They know "just saying no" is not an easy solution. The list of reasons not to use drugs is so long and so familiar that many teens just tune it out.

Teens are free thinkers. Many feel that what they do about drugs, legal or illegal, should be their own free choice. Most feel invincible. Who cares about warnings of wrinkles from smoking, or even those about lung cancer and emphysema? But they do care about their classmates who are strung out on drugs.

There is great energy for change among kids who have seen what drugs can do. Many of them know about the downside that follows the high. They respect the complicated and delicate working of their own brains, so they seek other highs that have more subtle and long-lasting rewards.

Thinkers want the facts, and as far as possible, facts have been presented in this book. They are more accurate than information from druggies on the street and pushers in the schools, where one in four claims to be able to buy marijuana in less than an hour.

At this very moment your brain is receiving countless messages. Some are conscious. Some are unconscious. Drugs change many messages in the brain and can change some of them permanently. Many of the kids who know this are in the forefront of the movement toward safer highs.

# Notes

CHAPTER 1

1. Susan Neiburg Terkel, *The Drug Laws: A Time for Change?* (New York: Franklin Watts, 1997), p. 102.

2. William Bennet, and others, *Body Count* (New York: Simon and Schuster, 1996), p. 156

3. National Household Survey on Drug Abuse, *The New York Times*, August 7, 1997.

4. National Institute on Drug Abuse Capsule, "Facts About Teen-agers and Drug Abuse," Monitoring the Future Survey, 1997.

5. "Survey Suggests Leveling Off In Use of Drugs by Students," *The New York Times*, December 21, 1997.

6. Christopher S. Wren, "Fewer Youths Report Smoking Marijuana," *The New York Times*, August 7, 1997.

7. Christopher S. Wren, "Drug Use by Young Teen-Agers Is Found Up," *The New York Times*, October 29, 1997.

CHAPTER 2

1. Lester Grispoon and James Bakalar in Raymond Goldberg, *Taking Sides: Drugs and Society* (Guilford, CT: Brown and Benchmark Publishers, 1996), p. 9.

2. Fred Leavitt, *Drugs and Behavior* (Thousand Oaks, CA: Sage, 1995), pp. 196-197.

3. Richard Seymour and David Smith, *Drugfree* (New York: Facts on File, 1987), p. 24.

4. *The Holy Bible*, King James Version, Genesis 9:20–21.

5. Margaret O. Hyde, *Alcohol: Uses and Abuses* (Hillside, NJ: Enslow, 1988), p. 15.

6. John Rublowsky, *The Stoned Age: A History of Drugs in America* (New York: Putnam, 1974), p. 58.

7. Rublowsky, pp. 57–73.

8. Andrew Weil and Winifred Rosen, *From Chocolate to Morphine: Everything You Need to Know About Mind Altering Drugs* (Boston: Houghton Mifflin, 1993), p. 83.

9. Rublowsky, pp. 118–122.

10. Marilyn Oliver, *Drugs: Should They Be Legalized?* (Springfield, NJ: Enslow, 1996), p. 11-12.

11. Jill Jonnes, *Hep-Cats, Narcs, and Pipe-Dreams: A History of America's Romance with Illegal Drugs* (New York: Scribners, 1996), pp. 42–43.

12. Rublowsky, p. 126.

13. Mathea Falco, *The Making of a Drug-Free America* (New York: Times Books, 1992), p.19.

14. Oliver, pp. 11–12.

15. Rublowsky, p. 123.

16. Rublowsky, p. 130.

17. Oliver, p. 19.

18. Jonnes, p. 190.

19. Falco, p. 19.

20. Roger Weiss and others, *Cocaine* (Washington, DC: American Psychiatric Press, 1994), p. 7.

21. Weil, p. 20.

22. Goldberg, p. 397.

23. Edward Brecher, *Licit and Illicit Drugs* (Boston: Little Brown, 1972), p. 416.

24. Weil, p. 115.

25. Brecher, p. 403.
26. Brecher, p. 400.
27. Brecher, pp. 408–409.
28. Jonnes, p. 130.
29. Jonnes, p. 255.
30. Brecher, p. 337.

CHAPTER 3

1. "LSD Makes a Comeback with Kids," *Christian Science Monitor*, February 20, 1996.
2. Darryl S. Inaba, William E. Cohen, and Michael E. Holstein, *Uppers, Downers, and All Arounders,* Third Edition (Ashland, OR: CNS Publications, 1997), p. 216.
3. Karen Bellenir, editor, *Substance Abuse Sourcebook* (Detroit: Omnigraphics, 1996), p. 347.
4. *Christian Science Monitor*, February 20, 1997.
5. Jennifer James, "Acid: LSD Today," (Tempe, AZ: D.I.N. Publications, 1996, pamphlet).

CHAPTER 4

1. "Chocolate May Mimic Drug, Study Says," *The New York Times*, August 22, 1997.
2. *Time*, May 5, 1997, pp. 69–76.
3. Barry Stimmel and the editors of Consumer Reports Books. *The Facts About Drug Use* (New York: The Haworth Medical Press, 1993), p. 190.
4. Stimmel, p. 104.
5. *Time*, May 5, 1997, p. 72.
6. Darryl S. Inaba, William E. Cohen, and Michael E. Holstein, *Uppers, Downers, and All Arounders,* Third Edition (Ashland, OR: CNS Publications, 1997), p. 103.
7. Inaba et al., p. 108.
8. "Drugs Had Big Role in Boy's Life, Death," *The Arizona Republic*, October 6, 1997.
9. The NCADI *Reporter*, June 30, 1997.
10. Stimmel, p. 179.

CHAPTER 5

1. Darryl S. Inaba, William E. Cohen, and Michael E. Holstein, *Uppers, Downers, and All Arounders,* Third Edition (Ashland, OR: CNS Publications, 1997), p. 159.

2. Robert O'Brien, Sidney Cohen, Glen Evans, and James Fine, *The Encyclopedia of Drug Abuse,* Second Edition (New York: Facts on File and Greenspring, Inc., 1992), p. 45.

3. O'Brien et al., p. 46.

4. O'Brien et al., p. 47.

5. Inaba et al., p. 166.

6. Inaba et al., pp. 170-171.

7. Barry Stimmel and the editors of Consumer Reports Books, *The Facts About Drug Use* (New York, The Haworth Medical Press, 1993), p. 106.

8. Stimmel, p. 105.

9. Stimmel, p. 101.

10. O'Brien et al., p. 260.

11. Inaba et al., p. 169.

12. O'Brien et al., p. 70.

13. Inaba et al., p. 144.

14. Inaba et al., p. 153.

15. A.M. Rosenthal, "Gone At Last," *The New York Times,* May 23, 1997.

CHAPTER 6

1. Darryl S. Inaba, William E. Cohen, and Michael E. Holstein, *Uppers, Downers, and All Arounders,* Third Edition (Ashland, OR: CNS Publications, 1997).

2. Wm. DeJong, "Prevention Pipeline," CASP, March/April 1997, p. 16.

3. Jill Jonnes, *Hep-Cats, Narcs, and Pipe-Dreams* (New York: Scribners, 1996), p.129.

4. Janice Phelps and Alan E. Nourse, *The Hidden Addiction and How to Get Free* (Boston: Little, Brown, 1986), p. 150.

5. Inaba et al., p. 20.

6. Phelps and Nourse, p. 157.

7. Lester Grispoon and James Bakalar, "Drug Abuse and Addiction," (Boston, MA: Harvard Mental Health Review, 1993), p. 31.

8. Grispoon and Bakalar, p. 30.

9. Richard Seymour and David E. Smith, *Drugfree* (New York: Facts on File, 1987), p. 59.

10. Inaba et al., p. 246.

11. Inaba et al., pp. 246–247.

12. Inaba et al., p. 246.

13. Phelps and Nourse, p. 152.

14. Grispoon and Bakalar, p. 32.

15. Phelps and Nourse, p. 252.

16. Grispoon and Bakalar, p. 31.

17. 1996 March Against Drugs Fact Sheet, p. 1.

18. Marijuana: Facts for Teens (Washington, DC: NIDA), p. 4.

19. *Science*, June 27, 1997, p. 1967.

20. Mark Gold, *The Facts About Drugs and Alcohol* (New York: Bantam Books, 1988), p. 71.

21. Grispoon and Bakalar, p. 32.

22. *Science*, June 27, 1997, pp. 1967–8.

23. Ibid., p. 1967.

24. Mathea Falco, *The Making of a Drug Free America* (New York: Times Books, 1992), p. 22.

25. Paul Armentano, "Weeding Through the Hype," NORML Report, 1996, p. 2.

26. Falco, p. 24.

27. Inaba et al., p. 236.

28. Susan Neiburg Terkel, *Should Drugs Be Legalized?* (New York: Franklin Watts, 1990), p. 54.

29. Inaba et al., p. 20.

30. Raymond Goldberg, *Taking Sides* (Guilford, CT: Brown and Benchmark Publishing Group, 1996), p. 138.

31. "Medical Marijuana Gets the High Sign," *Health*, November-December, 1996, p. 23.

## CHAPTER 7

1. Youth and Alcohol: An Overview, 1995, http://www.ncadd.org/youthalc.html

2. Darryl S. Inaba, William E. Cohen, and Micheal E. Holstein, *Uppers, Downers, and All Arounders,* Third Edition (Ashland, OR: CNS Publications, 1997), p. 202.

3. "Selling Alcohol Disguised as Punch," *The New York Times,* July 27, 1997.

4. Mothers Against Drunk Driving flyer, 1996.

5. Ibid., 1996.

6. Inaba et al., p. 196.

7. Inaba et al., p. 187.

8. Inaba et al., p. 186.

9. Inaba et al., pp. 191–195.

10. Inaba et al., p. 189.

11. Janice Phelps and Alan E. Nourse, *The Hidden Addiction and How to Get Free* (Boston: Little Brown, 1986), p. 93.

12. Debra Rosenberg and Matt Bai, "Drinking and Dying," *Newsweek,* October 13, 1997, p. 69.

13. Raymond Schroth, "Brotherhoods of Death," *America,* October 18, 1997, p. 6.

14. Ibana et al., p. 206.

15. Ibana et al., p. 186.

16. National Institute of Drug Abuse, "Prevention Pipeline," March/April, 1997, p. 32.

17. *Christian Science Monitor,* July 15, 1997.

18. University of Michigan, "Monitoring the Future," 1996.

19. Ibana et al., pp. 116-117.

20. Jack E. James, *Understanding Caffeine* (Thousand Oaks, CA: Sage, 1997), pp. 19–20.

21. "Caffeine's Cool Image Appeals to Kids, Perks Adult Concern," *Christian Science Monitor,* June 13, 1997.

22. Andrew Weil and Winifred Rosen, *From Chocolate to Morphine* (Boston: Houghton Mifflin, 1993), p. 41.

CHAPTER 8

1. Karin Swisher, *Legalizing Drugs* (San Diego: Greenhaven, 1996), p. 15.

2. Swisher, p. 59

3. Vincent Bugliosi, *The Phoenix Solution: Getting Serious About Winning America's Drug War* (Beverly Hills: Dove Books, 1996), p. 235.

4. Susan Neiburg Terkel, *The Drug Laws: A Time for Change?* (New York: Franklin Watts, 1997), p. 32.

5. "Free Heroin for Swiss," *The Arizona Republic*, September 29, 1997.

6. Susan Neiburg Terkel, *Should Drugs Be Legalized?* (New York: Franklin Watts, 1990), p. 13.

7. "Fewer Youths Report Smoking Marijuana," *The New York Times*, August 7, 1997.

8. "Drug Use by Teen-Agers Is Found Up," *The New York Times*, October 29, 1997.

9. Swisher, pp. 32–34.

10. www.norml.org/news/fax/archives/96-12-19-shtml, 1996

11. Terkel, *The Drug Laws*, p. 103.

12. "Capacity Building for Juvenile Substance Abuse Treatment," Washington, DC: National Criminal Justice Criminal Reference Service, Publication #167251. 1997.

13. Terkel, *The Drug Laws*, p. 50.

14. Mathea Falco, *The Making of a Drug-Free America* (New York: Random House, 1994), p. 8.

15. Falco, p. 177.

16. Falco, p. 176.

17. Raymond Goldberg, *Taking Sides* (Guilford, CT: Brown and Benchmark Publishers, 1996), p. 14.

18. Goldberg, p. 15.

19. Goldberg, pp. 5–6.

20. Terkel, *Should Drugs Be Legalized?*, p. 73.

21. Marilyn Oliver, *Drugs: Should They Be Legalized?* (Springfield, NJ: Enslow, 1996), p. 68.

22. Swisher, p 26.

23. Adam Gottlieb, *A Concise Encyclopedia of Legal Herbs and Chemicals with Psychoactive Properties* (Manhattan Beach, CA: 20th Century Alchemist, 1973), p. 1.

24. Swisher, p 71.

Chapter 9

1. Alan Y. Cohen, *Volunteerism and Community Service as Immunization Against Substance Abuse* (Bethesda, MD: Potomac Press, 1991).

2. Meher Baba, "The Place of Occultism in Spiritual Life: III," *Discourses* (San Francisco: Sufism Reoriented, 1967), Vol. 11, p. 110.

# Suggested Reading

Bailey, William Everett. *The Invisible Drug*. Houston: Mosaic Publications, 1996.

Bellener, Karen, Editor. *Substance Abuse Sourcebook*. Detroit: Omnigraphics, 1996.

Bennett, William J., John DiIulio, and John Walters. *Body Count: Moral Poverty and How to Win America's War Against Drugs and Crime*. New York: Simon and Schuster, 1996.

Falco, Mathea. *The Making of a Drug-Free America*. New York: Times Books, 1992.

Goldberg, Raymond, *Drugs and Society: Taking Sides*. Guilford, CT: Brown and Benchmark Publishers, 1996.

Hyde, Margaret O. *Know about Drugs*. Fourth Edition. New York: Walker, 1996.
———. *Know about Smoking*. Third Edition. New York: Walker, 1995.
———. *Mind Drugs*. Fifth Edition. New York: Putnam, 1986.

Inaba, Darryl S., William E. Cohen, and Michael E. Holstein. *Uppers, Downers, and All Arounders.* Third Edition. Ashland, OR: CNS Publications, 1997.

Jonnes, Jill. *Hep-Cats, Narcs, and Pipe-Dreams: A History of America's Romance with Illegal Drugs.* New York: Scribners, 1996.

Landau, Elaine. *Hooked: Talking About Addictions.* Brookfield, CT: Millbrook Press, 1994.

Leavitt, Fred. *Drugs and Behavior.* Thousand Oaks, CA: Sage Publications, 1995.

Lee, Mary Price, and Richard S. Lee. *Drugs and the Media.* New York: Rosen, 1994.

McLaughlin, Miriam Smith, and Sandra Peyser Hazouri. *Addiction: The "High" That Brings You Down.* Springfield, NJ: Enslow, 1997.

Myers, Arthur. *Drugs and Peer Pressure.* New York: Rosen, 1995.

Oliver, Marilyn Tower. *Drugs: Should They Be Legalized?* Springfield, NJ: Enslow, 1996.

Phelps, Janice Keller, and Alan E. Nourse. *The Hidden Addiction and How to Get Free.* Boston: Little, Brown, 1986.

Robbins, Paul R. *Hallucinogens.* Springfield, NJ: Enslow, 1996.

Rublowsky, John. *The Stoned Age: A History of Drugs in America.* New York: G. P. Putnam, 1974.

Seixas, Judith S. *Living with a Parent Who Takes Drugs.* New York: Greenwillow, 1989.

Seymour, Richard, and David E. Smith. *Drugfree: A Unique Positive Approach to Staying Off Alcohol and Other Drugs.* New York: Facts on File, 1987.

Simmel, Barry, and the Editors of Consumer Reports Books. *The Facts about Drug Use.* New York: The Haworth Medical Press, 1993.

Stares, Paul. *Global Habit.* Washington, DC: Brookings Institute, 1996.

Swisher, Karen, Editor. *Legalizing Drugs.* San Diego: Greenhaven, 1996.

Terkel, Susan Neiburg. *The Drug Laws: A Time for Change?* New York: Franklin Watts, 1997.

Wekesser, Carol, Editor. *Chemical Dependency: Opposing Viewpoints.* San Diego: Greenhaven, 1997.

Weil, Andrew, and Winifred Rosen. *From Chocolate to Morphine: Everything You Need to Know about Mind Altering Drugs.* Boston: Houghton Mifflin, 1993.

Weiss, Roger D., Stephen M. Mirin, and Roxanne L. Bartel. *Cocaine.* Washington, DC: American Psychiatric Press, 1994.

Winters, Paul A. *Teen Addiction.* San Diego: Greenhaven, 1997.

# Organizations

Al-Anon Family Groups
P.O. Box 862
New York, NY 10018
800-344-2666

American Council for Drug Education
204 Monroe Street, Suite 110
Rockville, MD 20850
800-488-DRUG

American Methadone Treatment Association
253–255 Third Avenue
New York, NY 10010

Cocaine Anonymous
3740 Overland Avenue, Suite G
Los Angeles, CA 90034
800-347-8998

DO IT NOW Foundation
Box 27568

Tempe, AZ 85285
602-736-0599

Mothers Against Drunk Driving
511 E. John Carpenter Freeway, Suite 700
Irving, TX 75062
214-744-6233

Narcotics Anonymous
World Service Office
P.O. Box 9999
Van Nuys, CA 01409
818-780-3951

National Association for Children of Alcoholics
31706 Coast Highway, Suite 201
South Laguna, CA 92677

National Clearinghouse for Alcohol and Drug Information
Box 2345
Rockville, MD 91409
800-729-6686

National Families in Action
2296 Henderson Mill Road, Suite 204
Atlanta, GA 30345
404–934-6364

National Federation of Parents for Drug-Free Youth
9551 Big Bend
St. Louis, MO 63122
314-968-1322

National Parents Resource Institute for Drug Education
(PRIDE)
The Hurt Building
50 Hurt Plaza, Suite 642
Atlanta, GA 30303
404-577-4500

# Hotlines

Center for Substance Abuse Treatment National Drug Hotline
800-662-HELP
Spanish-Speaking Callers:
800-66-AYUDA
This hotline, operated by the National Institute on Drug Abuse, is staffed Monday through Friday from 9 A.M. to 3 P.M. and from noon to 3 P.M. on Saturday and Sunday. Its purpose is to help drug users find and use local treatment programs, to provide support for "significant others," and provide drug-related information to the general public.

Cocaine Helpline
800-COCAINE
This hotline is operated 24 hours a day, 7 days a week.

National Council on Alcoholism
800-622-2255
This hotline is operated 24 hours a day, 7 days a week.

Look in your telephone directory's Yellow Pages under Alcoholism Information and Treatment Centers or Drug Abuse and Addiction Information for help in finding treatment near you.

# Websites

A large amount of information on alcohol, tobacco, and other mind drugs is available on the Internet. Some websites that may be helpful are listed below.

Families Against Mandatory Minimums (FAMM): www.famm.org/

Join Together Online: www.jointogether.org

The Marin Institute for the Prevention of Alcohol and Other Drug Problems: www.marininstitute.org

National Center on Addiction and Substance Abuse at Columbia University (CASA): www.casacolumbia.org

National Clearinghouse for Alcohol and Drug Information: www.health.org

National Families in Action Online: www.emory.edu/NFIA/

National Inhalant Prevention Coalition: www.inhalants.org

National Institute of Drug Abuse (NIDA): www.nida.nih.gov

National Organization for the Reform of Marijuana Laws: www.norml.org

Slang Terms from Drug-Free Resource Net: www.drugfreeamerica.org/slang.html

Substance Abuse and Mental Health Services Administration: www.samhsa.gov

# Street Terms: Drugs and the Drug Trade

If you hear talk about a drug, you can find out what that drug is by referring to a glossary of drug terms available by mail or on the web. It is important to know that if someone invites you to a rave, you can find out that it is a party designed to enhance a hallucinogenic experience through lights and music. If you are offered a "woolah," be aware that it is a hollowed cigar filled with marijuana and crack. If you hear someone talking about agonies, he or she may be referring to withdrawal.

A list of 2,300 street terms that refer to specific drug types and/or drug activity is available from the office of Drug Control Policy Information Clearinghouse, PO Box 6000, Rockville, MD 20849. It is available electronically through the ONDCP World Wide Web site. It can be viewed online or downloaded to your PC.

Point your browser to:

http://www.whitehousedrugpolicy.gov
Select "Drug Facts & Figures"
Select "Street Terms: Drugs and the Drug Trade"

# Index

Carter, Jimmy, 69
Catatonic syndrome, 30
Center for Substance Abuse
    Treatment National Drug
    Hotline, 122
"Chasing the dragon," 57
Chinese, 14, 16-17, 19
Chloral hydrate, 56
Chocolate, 38, 83
Cigarette smoking, 9, 38, 48,
    66, 73, 79-82, 97
Cigars, 81
Civil War, 17
Coca-Cola, 19
Cocaine, 9, 10, 18-19, 37-44,
    48, 68, 90
Cocaine Helpline, 122
Codeine, 18, 56
Coffee, 9, 38, 82, 83
Cola drinks, 82
Colonial America, 15
Crack (freebase), 10-12, 40, 42,
    90
Crank (see Methamphetamine)
Crashing, 43-44
Creative (aesthetic) level of
    experience, 103
Crime, 18, 91-92
Crystal (see Methamphetamine)

Darvon, 56
Decriminalization, 69, 71, 86
    (see also Legalization
    controversy)
Delusions, 25
Demerol, 18
Dendrites, 38
Depressants (see Downers)
Depression, 25, 30
Diet pills, 48
Dilated pupils, 27
Dopamine, 38-40, 53, 68
Downers, 49-59
    barbiturates, 50-53

benzodiazepines (BZDs),
    51, 53-55
Drug culture, 21
Drug testing, 93-94

Egyptians, 14, 16
Ehrenreich, Barbara, 92
Electroconvulsive treatments,
    26
Emotional level of experience,
    102
Epinephrine, 80

Fen-phen, 48
Fight or flight reaction, 41
Flashbacks, 28-30, 63
Flunitrazepam (Rohypnol),
    54
Formication, 41
Freeze and squeeze, 74
Freud, Sigmund, 19

Gamma aminobutyrate
    (GABA), 53
Gamma hydroxybutyrate
    (GHB), 55, 56
Gold, Mark, 67
Government regulation, 86
Greeks, 14, 16

Halcion, 53, 54
Hallucinogens, 23, 30 (see also
    LSD (lysergic acid diethyla-
    mide); Marijuana)
Harrison Narcotic Act of 1914,
    87
Hashish, 20, 96
Hepatitis, 42, 43
Heroin, 18, 38, 56-58, 86, 96
HIV (human immunodeficiency
    virus), 42, 43, 57, 67
Homer, 16
Hotlines, 122
"Huffing," 34, 36